To Act
According
to the Gospel

To Act
According
to the Gospel

XAVIER LÉON-DUFOUR

CHRISTOPHER R. SMITH, TRANSLATOR

© 2005 Hendrickson Publishers, Inc.
P. O. Box 3473
Peabody, Massachusetts 01961-3473

ISBN 1-56563-201-X

This is a translation of *Agir selon l'Évangile,* by Xavier Léon-Dufour. ©
Éditions du Seuil, Paris, 2002.

Printed in China

First Printing — June 2005

Cover Art: The cover photo is of an oil painting by Maurice Denis depict-
ing Jesus at the home of Mary and Martha as described in the gospel of
Luke. "Jesus chez Marthe et Marie (1ère pensée)," 1917. © 2005 Artists
Rights Society (ARS), New York/ADAGP, Paris. Photo Credit: Giraudon /
Art Resource, NY. Used with permission.

Library of Congress Cataloging-in-Publication Data

Léon-Dufour, Xavier.
    [Agir selon l'évangile. English]
    To act according to the Gospel / Xavier Léon-Dufour ;
translated by Christopher R. Smith.
        p. cm.
    Includes index.
    ISBN 1-56563-201-X (alk. paper)
    1. Christian life—Biblical teaching. 2. Bible. N.T. Gospels—
Theology. I. Title.
    BS2555.6.C48L4613 2005
    248.4—dc22
                              2005007700

Table of Contents

Foreword

Here I am, nearing old age and talking about action! But I do this in all good conscience. This work has actually grown out of a lifetime of experience. It is my attempt to realize a dream I have had since youth: to present the whole message of the gospel in such a way that it can be seen at a glance, so that readers may have at their disposal those gospel texts that should guide their spiritual lives. I want to enable them to respond better to the inner calling they may have already been hearing in secret.

When I first had this dream, the materials I would need were unfortunately separated into categories that made my exegetical inquiry almost impossible. My life circumstances led me to pursue the discipline of source criticism, as I was concerned to discover—and to make known—which of the gospel materials dated back to Jesus himself. Later, I entered the field of Johannine studies, where I could explore the transformation that the message of Jesus of Nazareth underwent very shortly after he lived. It might be more accurate to speak of its "transfiguration," because everything that was essential was retained,

but cast in a new light. The Synoptic tradition itself was made
new, without thereby losing its value or its significance.

Having realized this, I decided not to limit my inquiry to
how one should act in light of the teaching of Jesus of Nazareth,
but rather also to explore, each step of the way, how John had
transformed his teaching. I would like to chart a course that will
lead to a more faithful presentation of the gospel materials and,
ultimately, to a genuine "theology of the New Testament."

PRESUPPOSITIONS

It is appropriate for me to specify the commitments that
will direct the course of my reflections. I am conditioned by a
certain understanding of what humanity is. Intellectual hon-
esty demands that I not cut off all dialogue with my unbeliev-
ing friends here, but rather seek to deal with the objections that
will continually be raised concerning the validity of my enter-
prise. I say that God created humanity. But in what sense was it
created by God? How does one person relate to other people?
These are the questions we must first address.

The way God and the human person are currently represented needs to be modified considerably through a more at-
tentive reading of the biblical creation account. In this text,
God and the human person are not two mutually independent
beings, nor are people individuals who are set over against one
another. The universe is not a reality that exists by itself:

> When God began to create the heavens and the earth
> The earth was arid and empty,
> And darkness [was] on the surface of the deep;
> The breath of God hovered above the surface of the waters.
> (Gen 1:1, author's translation)

When read literally, the text does not say that we should understand the creative act as a divine production out of "nothing."

This concept of *ex nihilo* creation was no doubt developed to avoid making something exist "alongside" God. But does it not project onto our text the familiar myth of the "potter" God? (Gen 2:7).

It would be preferable to appeal here to a Jewish tradition, according to which the Hebrew verb *bara'* does not simply signify "create," in the sense of "produce," but rather derives from a root whose meaning is "expel outside." In this case God would have "expelled the creation outside himself," he would have "given birth" to the world by a creative expulsion.[1] This separation gives birth to a "non-God," a creature who acquires a real existence and subsists from then on by itself. It can thus accept or refuse the alliance that God proposes to make with it. If it accepts, it remains in relationship with God, by welcoming the One from whom it proceeds. To recognize myself as a creature is to affirm that God is the "Continuity" who supports my existence in all of its vagaries.

The second account of the formation of the first man shows the other relationship that constitutes humanity, the relationship with the soil and with the Spirit of God:

> The Lord God molded *'Adam*
> with some dust taken from the soil [*'adamah*].
> He breathed into his nostrils the breath of life [*nishmath khayyim*],
> and man became a living being [*lenefesh khayyah*].
> (Gen 2:7, author's translation)

This description must be correctly understood through the terms it uses. It establishes a relationship between *'Adam* (the human being) and *'Adamah* (the soil); by definition, the man is, according to his origins, terrestrial. His "body" is

---

[1] J. Eisenberg and A. Abecassis, *À Bible ouverte* (Albin Michel, 1991), 33.

close to the earth that he must cultivate,[2] according to the commandment:

> Be fruitful and multiply,
> And fill the earth and subdue it. (Gen 1:28)

The man received a mission from his creator: "act!" The location of his action was to be the soil.

This, then, is a second dimension of what it means to be human: it means to be a creature with the deepest affinity for the earth. But the human who has been created is still inert and only becomes "a living being" through the intervention of God, whom we know to be the "Living Being" par excellence:

> The Lord God . . . breathed into his nostrils the breath of life
> and the man became a living being. (Gen 2:7)

This statement is very frequently interpreted as referring to the "gift of life" in the form of a soul, a second element that constitutes the human person along with the body. But this interpretation does not take the original text sufficiently into account. The verb "breathed" comes from the same root (*nafakh*) as the term "nostril," so that the phrase actually reads "he breathed into the breath."[3] Or, to offer what seems to me a more readable paraphrase, the Lord "put his breath into" the dust. And what is this breath that the Lord God put in? The *nishmath khayyim* or "breath of life," which is called shortly afterward the *nishmath ruakh khayyim* (Gen 7:22), the "breath of the spirit of life." The term *neshamah* ("exhalation") is used here instead of *ruakh* ("breath" or "spirit"), probably to specify that the Lord does not "give" his "Spirit" as a thing, but that he breathes it in as an active principle of life.

---

[2] Gen 2:5.

[3] As in Ezekiel, where the Spirit must "breathe upon these slain, that they may live" (Ezek 37:9).

Thus God remains present, through his life-giving breath, with the human whom he created as a living being. When the passage is understood in this light, we realize that we should not speak of a separate substance in humans called the "soul." The soul is not an emanation from God any more than the body can be identified with the earth from whose dust it was drawn.

But then what are the soul and the body? Let me hazard a suggestion:

> *The body is the earth in which I participate even now.*
> *The soul is the Spirit of God in which I participate even now.*

This analysis has numerous implications. The human person is a single being, uniting within itself the breath of life and the dust from which it is drawn. There are not two co-principles within the human person that we can call "soul" and "body." Thus, in keeping with Hebrew anthropology, my "soul" is not immortal by nature; when I die, I cease to live entirely, because the breath of God returns to God, leaving the dust inert. But my soul brings with it my history, that which I have written with God. The cries of the psalmist make sense in this perspective.

However, it would not be fair to impute to the Jews the belief that at death the human person returns to nothingness. They believed instead that all the dead descended to a place called "Sheol," a place of silence, inhabited by "shadows." Unlike the Egyptians, the Hebrews did not indulge the idea of some imaginary afterlife; they thought instead that God could give them the gift of a full life. They retained between themselves and God a real connection that I call "existence": at death, I have no more body through which to express myself, but through my history I continue to exist in God, who caused me to be. We may sum all of this up by saying: *when I die, I cease to live, but not to exist.*

Nevertheless, this anthropology only becomes Christian when it includes as well what is known as faith in the "resurrection." To conceive this as the resuscitation of a body that has become a corpse would be to presuppose that death is the separation of the soul and the body, an opinion that is difficult to reconcile with the Bible, which maintains a unity of soul and body and recognizes no "existence" of the dead other than in God. The "resurrection" of the soul-body ensemble consists rather in the definitive life that God will grant in the end.[4]

The human as a living being is therefore defined by his relationship *with God by whom he lives* and *with the earth by which he expresses himself,* that is, with the flowers and with the animals, but essentially with other humans. The first man was defined most particularly with the woman who was given to him as a counterpart:

> Elohim created Adam in his image,
> In the image of Elohim he created him,
> He created them male and female.
> (Gen 1:27, author's translation)

Would Adam therefore include both man and woman? Adam is actually not, properly speaking, an individual—he represents humanity as a whole. Perhaps this is the reason why he does not speak until he recognizes Eve: he only becomes an individual when he enters into dialogue with her, recognizing thereby that woman is the quintessence of man. Every human being is sexual and must exclaim in the presence of the other:

> This at last is bone of my bones and flesh of my flesh!
> (Gen 2:23)

---

[4] If space had permitted, I would have drawn more extensively on my essay *Résurrection de Jésus et Message Pascal,* 5th ed. (Paris: Seuil, 1971).

Human life, therefore, is stirred up by the presence of an Other. I only become myself in recognizing this Other as a new "myself." "My neighbor is other than me, an other who can remain 'another' to me, but who can also become a brother, that is, another 'myself.'"[5]

---

[5] See my article "Prochain" ["Neighbor"] in *VTB*, 1038.

Abbreviations

Books of the Bible

Gen	Genesis
Exod	Exodus
Lev	Leviticus
Num	Numbers
Deut	Deuteronomy
Judg	Judges
1–2 Sam	1–2 Samuel
Ps(s)	Psalm(s)
Prov	Proverbs
Eccl	Ecclesiastes
Isa	Isaiah
Jer	Jeremiah
Ezek	Ezekiel
Dan	Daniel
Zech	Zechariah
Sir	Sirach (Ecclesiasticus)
Tob	Tobit
Wis	Wisdom
Matt	Matthew

Rom	Romans
1–2 Cor	1–2 Corinthians
Gal	Galatians
Eph	Ephesians
Col	Colossians
1–2 Thess	1–2 Thessalonians
Heb	Hebrews
1–2 Pet	1–2 Peter

General

DNT	Léon-Dufour, Xavier. *Dictionnaire du Nouveau Testament.* 3d ed. Paris: Seuil, 1996. An English translation of the second edition is available: Léon-Dufour, Xavier. *Dictionary of the New Testament.* Translated by T. Prendergast. San Francisco: Harper & Row, 1980
Merklein	Helmut Merklein, *Die Gottesherrschaft als Handlungsprinzip. Untersuchung zur Ethik Jesu.* 3d ed. Würzburg: Echter Verlag, 1984
RSR	*Recherches de science religieuse*
Str-B	Strack, Hermann L., and Paul Billerbeck. *Kommentar zum Neuen Testament aus Talmud und Midrasch.* 6 vols. Munich: C. H. Beck, 1922–1961
TOB	*Traduction oecuménique de la Bible.* 2d ed. Paris: Alliance biblique universelle-Cerf, 1991
VTB	Léon-Dufour, Xavier. *Voçabulaire de théologie biblique.* 2d ed. Paris: Cerf, 1970. An English edition is available: Léon-Dufour, Xavier. *Dictionary of Biblical Theology.* Translated by P. J. Cahill. London: Chapman, 1973
YHWH	The consonants in Yahweh, the revealed name of God

Introduction

"We are born to act," said Montaigne. This is a truth of our experience that each one of us will recognize. Every person is animated instinctively from youth by the drive to discover, to procreate, to transform the world. Even when, later in life, we are constrained by weaknesses that reduce us to inactivity, we are still characterized by a desire that would drive us to act if we could.

The philosopher Maurice Blondel elaborated the deep structure of this "action" a hundred years ago. There is no need to repeat his work. For their part, "moralists" have striven to describe the conditions of a good or a bad action and to specify what our manner of acting should be. Different ethical systems seek to identify the criteria of human action, by referring either to a past that is considered normative (such as "Thou shalt not kill . . .") or to a future that promises a reward on this earth (as in the Marxist perspective) or beyond this earth (as in the Bible). The goal we will be pursuing here is to dig even deeper, right down to the very root of human action according to the gospel.

Because I presuppose, in keeping with my anthropology, that each person depends upon an "Other," my work will be addressed to everyone who is not closed in upon oneself but remains open to an Other, who does not necessarily have to be called "God," even if, for my part, I will call him that.

Beyond this, since I believe that Jesus Christ is God's mediator, I will also be addressing myself to a narrower audience, whom I invite to deepen their faith by listening to the words of Jesus and by discovering his character through his actions. He is the type of person that all Christians are called to be.

Finally, recognizing that Jesus of Nazareth did not impose ready-made truths on his contemporaries but was content simply to raise the question of his person—"But you, who do you say that I am?"[1]—I would suggest that in discovering what Jesus' manner of acting was, readers raise for themselves the question of how one should act.

I therefore have three different kinds of readers in mind: those who are open to an Other, those who are Christians and would like to deepen their faith, and finally those who are nonbelievers.

One primary presupposition of our study should be examined briefly. Why should the action of every person be modeled after that of Jesus of Nazareth, and appeal thereby be made to the Christian faith? The basis of this believing inquiry is that Jesus, the God-man, is Humanity par excellence. He did not simply enunciate which attitudes should characterize his disciples; his own behavior represented their actualization. The teaching and counsel he gave to his disciples flowed from his own experience. He did not present himself as a

---

[1] This is the question I as a historian have recognized myself to have been asking, at the end of a long inquiry into the text of the gospels. See my work *Les évangiles et l'histoire de Jésus* (10th ed; Paris: Seuil, 1990), 490.

legislator or as a teacher of morals; he came like a charismatic prophet and drew followers in his wake. We cannot therefore ask him for "norms," because these would be dead apart from their context, and trying to follow them would be the death of liberty. But the analogous situation of our world does legitimize drawing applications to our own time.

Every inquiry into the gospels requires a method. Historians begin by examining the first three gospels: Matthew, Mark, and Luke—that is, the Synoptic tradition. They believe that in this way they can get back to the "Jesus of history." The method by which they seek to do this (with which exegetes will already be familiar) is a development of nineteenth-century gospels research. According to the "Two-Source Theory," Matthew and Luke derive from Mark and an ancient source called Q (from *Quelle,* the German word for "source"), which can be reconstructed from those materials not found in Mark that are common to Matthew and Luke. Critics believe that by using the Two-Source Theory they can reach a tradition that predates the gospels, prior to Christian reinterpretation.

Two principles govern their research. According to the first, that of "difference," that which cannot be attributed to the early Christian community is recognized to have come from Jesus. When, for example, Jesus commands his disciples, "Go nowhere among the Gentiles, and enter no town of the Samaritans" (Matt 10:5), this formulation is definitely from Jesus. Given that the early Christians quickly began to preach the gospel to both Samaritans and Gentiles, how could the early church have put a commandment in Jesus' mouth that the disciples immediately disobeyed?

Along with this negative criterion, another is also employed, that of "coherence" with the words one feels confident Jesus truly spoke. For example, in the Gospel of Mark, Jesus quotes a prophecy of Zechariah to support his declaration to the disciples that they would all abandon him at the time of his passion: "You will all become deserters; for it is written, 'I will strike the shepherd, and the sheep will be scattered'" (Mark 14:27). Other than in his controversies with the Pharisees, however, Jesus never justified himself by a scriptural text, because he is the master of the Scriptures. The conclusion therefore seems unavoidable that this precise formulation does not come from Jesus of Nazareth. However, we can recognize that it nevertheless expresses the word of Jesus quite profoundly. The early Christians knew that Jesus must have said something along these lines; not having the exact wording, they found in the Bible this phrase that uses Jesus' familiar terms of the shepherd and the flock. By following this method, it is believed, we can get back to the action of Jesus through those sayings that may truly be deemed "historical."

While I acknowledge the value of such an inquiry, I do not think we should be entirely content with it. It is appropriate to point out a possible excess of this so-called historico-critical method: if we are too confident that we have recovered the actual wording of the authentic sayings of Jesus, we risk undervaluing words that are sometimes too hastily dismissed as a product of the early Christian community.

Indeed, sayings that are believed not to have come from Jesus himself can nevertheless clarify the meaning of the bare skeleton unearthed by the historian. This presumes that we will not be content to use only the critical scalpel, but that we will see the genuine value of the tradition that conveys the "historical" saying. Our understanding of the meaning of "sayings" that are considered genuine can be helpfully informed by an appreciation of their gospel settings. We will demonstrate this in the course of our study of the first saying of Jesus recorded in the Gospel of Mark.

We are thus led to examine the data of the Fourth Gospel as well, even though it constantly transforms the affirmations of the Synoptics. Interpreters of this gospel freely acknowledge it to be a product of the early church. Nevertheless, the church has proclaimed its canonicity, its place within the official corpus of texts accepted as inspired. The good news has therefore come to us not only in the Synoptics, but through four gospels. Together they constitute the Gospel with a capital G, meaning that the good news cannot be reduced to any one of the four writings that transmit it.

This is why I have abandoned my initial project on "The action of humanity according to Jesus of Nazareth" and am proposing instead: "Acting according to the Gospel."

Our inquiry will proceed in five stages:

1. The experience of Jesus: God is present, he is coming, he is here.

2. The criterion of action: not the law, but God alone.

3. The human person in relation to God-who-is-coming.

4. The human person in relation to the universe: the earth, the Other.

5. Love at the heart of action.

Chapter 1

The Fundamental Experience
of Jesus

ACCORDING TO THE SYNOPTIC TRADITION
God is present, he has come to reign, he is here

As we read through the gospel narratives, we find the person of Jesus admirable, both for his words and for his actions. We wonder where he got his remarkable capabilities. Can we find a thread that will lead to their origins? What was the power source of his activity? Theologies of the New Testament typically seek to answer this question by developing a theme that is assumed to lie at the heart of Jesus' message.

But our task is not simply to identify some essential principle that the Synoptic Gospels reveal, such as "God is Father." Certainly we learn from these gospels that Jesus called God his "Father," even addressing God as "Abba."[1] They also disclose the unique understanding Jesus had of the Father.[2] The Lord's

---

[1] Mark 14:36.
[2] Luke 10:21; Matt 11:25–27.

Prayer, in which God is addressed as "Our Father," was certainly intended as a model for the believer.[3] Nevertheless, the Synoptic Gospels—by contrast with the Fourth Gospel—do not present this as the center of Jesus' message.

The majority of New Testament interpreters propose instead that the concept of the "reign of God" lies at the center of Jesus' thought. This is our own understanding as well, although we would specify that this concept is what principally *reveals* the thought of Jesus.

The gospel texts present the saying that "the reign of God has come near" as the heart of the message the disciples were to transmit. They treat it as a summary of that message. We will therefore conduct a rigorous analysis of this message, "God is reigning right now," and then explore the nature of his urgent and mysterious presence.[4]

The Text of Mark 1:15

After specifying that Jesus began his ministry after John the Baptist was arrested, Mark summarizes his preaching in a pregnant phrase:

> [14]He proclaimed the good news of God [15]and said, "The time is fulfilled and the reign of God has come near; repent, and believe in the good news." (Mark 1:14–15, NRSV, var.)

In this summary, the evangelist uses phrases that seem to be derived from several different contexts. In saying that Jesus "proclaimed the good news of God," he is speaking as a member of the Christian community announcing the good news

---

[3] Matt 6:9–13.

[4] This first study, while fundamental to all that follows, will make for the most difficult reading. Readers who prefer to avoid the subtleties of exegetical inquiry are invited to skip to the section "The Reign of God Has Landed Right on Top of You," p. 16.

that God made known through the One he sent (1 Thess 2:2, 8–9). When, in Mark's gospel, Jesus says "the time is fulfilled," he does not use the term *chronos,* which expresses a certain length of time, such as that of a day or a year, but rather the term *kairos* (more typical in this gospel). It refers to a specific moment that must be discerned in the flux of history; for which you must "keep alert, for you do not know when the time will come."[5] When he invites people to *be converted,* he is speaking like the author of the Acts of the Apostles, which continually associates proclamation with conversion.[6] Jesus, however, did not elaborate a theology of conversion; from his perspective, conversion did not have the same meaning as for John the Baptist. For John, conversion meant forsaking a life of sin, while for Jesus it meant hearing the good news[7] and receiving a joy that nothing could take away.[8] These varying expressions all appear to reflect the language of the early church rather than that of Jesus of Nazareth.

However, it seems very likely that the second statement in Mark's summary expresses the experience of Jesus himself. In

---

[5] Mark 13:33; cf. 11:13; 12:2. I do not see a Pauline influence here, despite Merklein, 19, and Jacques Schlosser, *Le règne de Dieu dans les dits de Jésus* (Paris: Gabalda, 1980), 100. Paul actually speaks of the "times" (*chronoi*) being accomplished (Gal 4:4, Eph 1:10).

[6] Acts 2:38; 3:19; 11:18; 19:4; 26:20.

[7] Luke makes the call to conversion a corporate one (Luke 10:13 and pars.; 11:32 and pars.; 13:3, 5; 15:7, 10). Cf. Helmut Merklein, "Die Umkehrpredigt bei Johannes dem Täufer und Jesus von Nazaret," *Biblische Zeitschrift* 25 (1981): 29–46 [*Studein zu Jesus und Paulus* (Tübingen: Mohr, 1987), 119].

[8] "How beautiful upon the mountains are the feet of the messenger who announces peace, who brings good news, who announces salvation, who says to Zion, 'Your God reigns.' Listen! Your sentinels lift up their voices, together they sing for joy; for in plain sight they see the return of the Lord to Zion" (Isa 52:7–8; Matt 2:10; Luke 2:10).

the middle of v. 15 comes the major announcement: "The reign of God has come near." New Testament interpreters as a whole judge this to be an authentic saying of Jesus. One assertion stands out: God has drawn near. But ever since God revealed himself to Abraham, he had constantly presented himself as the One who was with Israel. Hence we are led to ask: in what way was the nearness of God that Jesus proclaimed something new?

When Jesus sent out the Twelve (as reported in the source Q), he instructed them to offer peace and to heal the sick, and he told them to proclaim his message:

> As you go, proclaim that the reign of God has come near. (Matt 10:7 = Luke 10:9, 11,[9] NRSV, var.)

Even if one phrase or another of the Mission Discourse may not be strictly attributable to Jesus, this formula reflects his thought. This is clearly how Mark understood that thought, as evidenced by the first saying he attributes to Jesus, in a summary of his preaching at the time when "after John was arrested Jesus came to Galilee" (1:14). The object of our inquiry will be to discover what Jesus meant by this affirmation.

Semantic Study of the Expression "Reign of God"

We will use the formulation "reign of *God,*" which Mark and Luke customarily employ, rather than that of Matthew, who writes "reign of *heaven.*" Interpreters generally agree that Matthew, in keeping with the rabbinic practice of never naming God directly, preferred to resort to a current metaphor, "heaven."[10]

---

[9] The *Traduction œcuménique de la Bible* unfortunately translates Luke's version as "has arrived."

[10] R. Schnackenburg, *Règne et Royaume de Dieu* (Paris: L'Orante, 1965), 67–68, argues for such an interpretation. Mark and Luke wished to avoid any misunderstanding on the part of their Hellenistic

In English,[11] depending on the context, two different terms, "reign" and "kingdom," must be used to translate the single Greek expression *basilea tou theou*. We should specify their respective connotations.

The phrase "reign of God" presents, in a Semitic framework, the mysterious reality of God reigning, that is, God at work in the world of humans, specifically in their favor. The dynamism suggested in this phrasing is confirmed by the fact that the expression is often associated with a verb of movement: "has come near,"[12] "has come,"[13] "come,"[14] "has come."[15] God's activity cannot be observed[16] and is like a seed growing secretly, or a tiny seed that becomes a great tree, or leaven in dough.[17]

The phrase "kingdom of God" designates the result of the divine action toward humanity; consequently, unlike the "reign," it is a future entity. It is the horizon to which those of the Jewish faith are encouraged to look; it is a good that one "seeks," something into which one "desires to enter" or even "forces one's way."[18] The notion of a "kingdom" can lead to

---

readers, although sometimes they felt free to use the term "heaven" (Mark 11:30–31; Luke 15:7, 18, 21). Matthew, for his part, does not hesitate to speak of "the kingdom" (4:23; 8:12; 9:35; 13:19, 38; 24:14), while Luke only mentions it three times (12:32; 22:29; Acts 20:25).

[11] The author actually discusses the two French terms *règne* and *royaume,* which correspond to *reign* and *kingdom,* respectively. — Trans.

[12] Mark 1:15; Luke 10:9, 11.

[13] Mark 9:1; Luke 11:2.

[14] Matt 6:10; Mark 14:25; Luke 22:18.

[15] Luke 11:20.

[16] Luke 17:20.

[17] Mark 4:26–29; 4:30–32; Luke 13:20–21.

[18] Luke 12:32; 16:16; Mark 9:47.

misunderstandings: Israel in Jesus' day assimilated it to the idea of the Messiah coming to establish the earthly rule of their nation. In a similar way Christians have sometimes mistakenly identified the kingdom with the church.[19]

Our particular interest will be in those cases where the translation "reign of God" is appropriate, where the expression presents in a Semitic framework the concrete reality of God reigning. The experience of Jesus was that the reign of God was already under way.

History of the Expression

Jesus spoke of the "reign of God" as the heir of a long Jewish tradition. The experience of the exodus and the sojourn in the wilderness led to the recognition not that a certain territory belonged to God, but that God acted within history: "The Lord will reign forever and ever!"[20] After a long study, Schnackenburg has affirmed, "The idea of the kingship of God has its roots in many different strata of the Old Testament; it goes back to the earliest days of the religion of Israel. God reigns over creation, over Israel and over the nations, although in different ways and to different degrees."[21] This belief was expressed in Israel's worship, particularly in the enthronement psalms:[22] "Yes! God is King!" With the prophets (who appealed to other images as well, particularly that of the Shepherd), the eschatological dimension of God's kingship over Israel first appeared, particularly in Second Isaiah,[23] who

---

[19] This is something that Schnackenburg wisely warned against as early as 1958 (*Règne,* 293–96).

[20] Exod 15:18; cf. 1 Sam 12:12; Ps 145:11–12; 146:10.

[21] Schnackenburg, *Règne,* 19–34.

[22] Pss 47–93; 96; 99.

[23] Isa 24:23; 33:22; 43:15; 44:6; 52:7.

introduced a new figure, the Servant of God. Finally the religious image of a Messiah-King emerged.[24]

In the two centuries before Jesus, under the pressure of successive foreign occupations, the hope developed of a messianic kingdom in Israel, as the request of the sons of Zebedee for places of honor in the coming kingdom shows,[25] and as various apocryphal writings of the period also show, for example, the Psalms of Solomon, or the eleventh of the Eighteen Prayers, or even the Kaddish: "May he give reign to his kingship!" Little by little, the eschatological aspect of this expectation, in which God would reign over the whole world, began to prevail, especially in apocalyptic literature (for example, the book of Daniel and the *Parables of Enoch*). Wisdom of Solomon extends to righteous people everywhere the right to participate in the final kingdom: "At the time of the last judgment . . . they will judge the peoples, they will rule over the nations, and the Lord will be their king forever."[26] This was the character of the eschatological reign of God that the Jews in the time of Jesus, especially the Zealots, were expecting: universal but terrestrial.[27] For their part, Christians have always hoped for a reign of similar extent: "Thy kingdom come!"[28]

Until then, believers can, through their faith in God, live under God's reign, because the kingdom takes shape everywhere that people allow the action of Jesus Christ—which is the action of God-who-reigns—to take place through them.

---

[24] Zech 9:9.

[25] Mark 10:37.

[26] Wis 3:7–8.

[27] *Jubilees* 1:28.

[28] Luke 11:2 and pars. [While the author has *règne* here instead of *royaume,* I have used the familiar English phrase. This seems appropriate even within the author's discussion, given that a future expectation is being expressed.—Trans.]

This was Jesus' message and his contemporaries could have understood it. But they did not, as we will see when we take this theme up again in chapter 3.

The Reign of God Has Come Near

By announcing that the reign of God had already come near, Jesus took a position that challenged the popular belief. What, then, was this proximity of which he spoke? The Greek verb *engizein* signifies "to draw near."[29] Protesting justifiably against those critics who imprudently disallowed any actualization of the reign of God, C. H. Dodd[30] proposed that Mark 1:15 should be translated, "the reign of God *has arrived*." He justified this translation by assimilating this phrase to the preceding one, "the time is fulfilled." But these two statements are not equivalent. Saying that "the time is fulfilled" means that a point in time has been reached, while saying that the reign of God is imminent means that a period of time is about to begin. Affirming that it is already here, with nothing more to follow, fails to recognize that God does not yet reign completely in the world.

Even though he retained an eschatological expectation, Jesus did not think the coming of God to reign would occur only in the last days. He thus added a new dimension onto this expectation. He did not say in what sense, or when, or how God was just about to reign; he simply affirmed that we needed to remain alert to welcome him, however he might present

---

[29] Locally (Matt 11:1) or temporally (Matt 21:1; Luke 21:8) or metaphorically (Rom 13:12).

[30] C. H. Dodd, *Les Paraboles du royaume de Diu. Déjà là ou pas encore* (Paris: Seuil, 1977), 44. This assertion drew protests from many critics, including W. C. Kummel, N. Perrin, and R. Schnackenburg, who argued that the event had occurred, but that its realization had not yet been achieved (Schnackenburg, *Règne,* 118).

himself. If we do not yet take up the later declaration that the reign has come (Luke 11:20), we will be able to retain the sense of hope and expectation, even if its object is not specified.

When we consider this summary of Jesus' message, therefore, we find that it doesn't spell everything out for us; it rather leaves us in suspense. There is clearly more to come, but what? The answer is not given here, but it does emerge in the course of the gospel narratives, where we hear about the unlimited forgiveness that God extends. Nevertheless there is a suggestion of it even here, in the immediate context, in the contrast with the preaching of John the Baptist.

The Message of Jesus Compared with That of the Precursor

Mark places his introduction of the ministry of Jesus right after the announcement made by the Precursor. Matthew and Luke have each added a sample of John's preaching that has been preserved by the source Q. Matthew has even drawn a parallel between the two figures by lending to John the same proclamation about the reign of God:

Repent, for the kingdom of heaven has come near. (Matt 3:2)

By contrast, the actual preaching of John helps us grasp the sense of Jesus' own preaching:

You brood of vipers! Who warned you to flee from the wrath to come? [8]Bear fruit worthy of repentance. [9]Do not presume to say to yourselves, "We have Abraham as our ancestor"; for I tell you, God is able from these stones to raise up children to Abraham. [10]Even now the ax is lying at the root of the trees; every tree therefore that does not bear good fruit is cut down and thrown into the fire. [11]I baptize you with water for repentance, but one who is more powerful than I is coming after me; I am not worthy to carry his sandals. He will baptize you with the

Holy Spirit and fire. [12]His winnowing fork is in his hand, and he will clear his threshing floor and will gather his wheat into the granary; but the chaff he will burn with unquenchable fire. (Matt 3:7–12)

These words of John are striking in their severity: There must be repentance; there is no other recourse; descent from Abraham counts for nothing. The heavens are closed; they will only open with the coming of Jesus (3:16), whom John says to expect not so much as the one who will bring some kind of salvation, but rather as the agent of God's terrible and imminent wrath. John declares that God's judgment will fall upon a sinful Israel, and he offers a baptism of repentance by which one may escape this wrath and be prepared to welcome the one who comes as judge.

The figure of Jesus stands over against this terrible tableau, simply announcing the good news that God has now come to reign. He will joyfully inaugurate a new regime, whose character the Messiah will disclose by his acts and his teaching. By giving no further specifics here, Jesus leaves the future open: the reign of God has come near! If there is mention of repentance, this comes not before but after the good news has been proclaimed.

The message of Jesus thus leaves the hearer in suspense. It makes us dream of the future, but above all it invites us to stay alert, in the expectation of a stunning intervention of God. As readers we are held in this attitude and ask ourselves what's going to happen. Let's not rush to the answer, but just remain expectant.

The Reign of God Has Landed Right on Top of You

The answer will make itself known in various ways, for example, through the parables of the reign, or in the Beatitudes, which declare that the kingdom of God belongs to the poor. It will become clearer throughout the whole life of Jesus. While we wait, let us continue to concentrate on the announcement of the reign of God, whose coming is said to be near, or which is even affirmed to be present.

Indeed, besides the announcements of an imminent reign, there is another saying, which critics judge to have come from Jesus himself, which affirms that the reign is *already present*. This saying, transmitted by both Luke and Matthew, vividly illuminates the scope of the reign as Jesus understood it. It is preceded in Luke by a significant episode:

> [17]The seventy-two returned [from their mission] with joy, saying, "Lord, in your name even the demons submit to us!" [18][Jesus] said to them, "I watched Satan fall from heaven like a flash of lightning." (Luke 10:17–18, NRSV, var.)

The joy of triumph resounds in this exchange. Jesus effectively moves beyond the simple proximity of the reign to proclaim its realization. And from his own exorcisms, he drew the lesson:

> No one can enter a strong man's house and plunder his property without first tying up the strong man; then indeed the house can be plundered. (Mark 3:27)

This is considered an "authentic" saying of Jesus, since it comes from the earliest sources. We can verify its meaning by studying more closely the Q-source in Luke and Matthew:

> [14][Jesus] was casting out a demon that was mute; when the demon had gone out, the one who had been mute spoke, and the crowds were amazed. [15]But some of them said, "He casts out demons by Beelzebul, the ruler of the demons." . . . [17]But he knew what they were thinking and said to them, "Every kingdom divided against itself becomes a desert, and house falls on house. [18]If Satan also is divided against himself, how will his kingdom stand?—for you say that I cast out the demons by Beelzebul. [19]Now if I cast out the demons by Beelzebul,

by whom do your exorcists cast them out? Therefore they will
be your judges. [20]But if it is by the finger of God that I cast
out the demons, then the reign of God has come to you
[*ephthasen*]." (Luke 11:14–20, NRSV, var. = Matt 12:22–28)

In noting that, at his word, demons are expelled, Jesus
recognizes that through him God is triumphing over the Adversary, over "Satan."[31] Let us specify the meaning of the terms
used in v. 20. The implications of Jesus' work have been revealed to him, and he explains them here. "Has come upon
you" is from the verb *phthanō* ("to arrive"), with a nuance of
"falling right on top of," with a startling impact. When he says
"by the finger of God," Jesus is making an allusion to the text
of Exodus, where the magicians of Egypt admit that they have
been beaten by the plague of gnats: "This is the finger of
God!"[32] (Exod 8:19).

Jesus reasons here in a way that should satisfy our legitimate, rational expectations. Observing that the demons have
been defeated by himself and by his disciples, he draws a conclusion from this fact: God is victoriously at work against the
powers of evil. The adverb "then"[33] makes the connection between the observation and the deduction. Mark describes the
victory over the strong man, in other words, over Satan (cf. Isa
49:24–25; 53:12). Luke speaks explicitly of Beelzebul, one of
the names of the prince of demons (Job 1:6).

The difference between an imminent reign and a reign
that has already arrived may appear to be a contradiction. But
it can be explained, and this explanation may even suggest a

---

[31] See *DNT,* 144, 491–92. See also my essay "Que diable!"
Études (March 2002): 349–63.

[32] Bernard Couroyer makes this observation in "Le 'droigt de
Dieu' (Exode 8:15)," *Revue biblique* 63 (1956): 481–95.

[33] *Ara* in Luke; cf. 11:48; cf. Paul: 2 Cor 5:14; Gal 2:21; 3:29;
5:11; Heb 12:8; *kai tote* in Mark 13:27.

compatibility between the two declarations. The victory over the depths of evil personified in demons is understood by Jesus as a sovereign act of God, whose reality manifests itself among people through his own supremacy over the Adversary in exorcisms, such as that among the Gerasenes (Mark 5:11–20) or of the possessed man who was mute (Matt 9:32–34), or even through the stilling of the storm (Mark 4:36–41). To speak in mythical terms, Satan must be dispossessed before the intervention of God can find its way among people. But this intervention itself depends on the welcome it must freely receive.

At the same time, the witnesses of what Jesus was enabled to do had to have recognized what he represented, and from whom he received his power. In many Jewish texts, the object of God is to triumph over Satan.[34]

According to the gospels, there was another amazing way in which Jesus demonstrated the radical renewal that flowed from extending a welcome to God, who was coming. This is the meaning of his miracles of healing (such as at Capernaum, Mark 2:1–12). True, many critics consider these accounts of miraculous works to be relics of an antiquated way of thinking. Certain psychological forces, they insist, are capable of bringing on the kinds of illnesses that in those days were attributed to demons. However, even if we do not have medical proof that Jesus' healings were genuine, we must still acknowledge, at least in a general sense, the existence of phenomena such as the gospels report.[35]

---

[34]Cf. H. Kruse, "Das Reich Satans," *Biblica* 58 (1977): 29–61. God is victor over the empire of Satan as well as over evil. See also Schlosser, *Le règne de Dieu,* 134–38.

[35]Allow me to refer the reader to an anthology, Jean-Noël Aletti and Xavier Léon-Dufour, *Les miracles de Jésus selon le Nouveau Testament* (Paris: Seuil, 1977).

What interests us above all is the observation that Jesus of Nazareth was fully conscious of triumphing over the Adversary of God's design. He was therefore not content simply to announce that the reign of God was imminent; he accompanied his words with deeds that signified that God was actively present at that moment, and thus that God desired to renew the covenant. These actions, which one might term "symbolic," *are and are not* God at work: by expelling demons, Jesus restored health—that is, he extended forgiveness and salvation.

Besides these references to combat (or, more accurately, to victory), Jesus described positively the new state he was inaugurating by identifying those who belonged to the reign of God: the poor, whom he declared blessed.

In the first saying of Jesus (Mark 1:15), the reign is imminent. In the second (Matt 12:28), it is presently at work. Different verbs are used, *engiken* and *ephthasen,* respectively, with only the latter having the nuance of "to have already arrived" and even "to land on top of." Jesus now has the experience of God at work. This work does not consist in establishing the "kingdom," but in ending Satan's domination.

As Jesus himself was the author of these divine manifestations, those who saw them could recognize that Jesus was acting personally in place of God. Little by little, the early Christians therefore substituted for the "reign of God" a "Christology," which was solidly reinforced by the resurrection appearances.

Questions of Language

This talk of a "reign," when applied to God, may present difficulties for modern readers, for whom the image of a "reign" may suggest an autocratic monarch. These difficulties are inherent in the way God revealed himself to the chosen people. The history of the kings of Israel shows that Samuel was right to warn of the dangers of the monarchy the people wanted: would it not end up supplanting the kingship that was rightfully God's alone (1 Sam 8)? In our day, when it is taken for granted that "democracy" should be the form of government, the language of kingship must be handled delicately, even if it really means "God-who-reigns." Everything really depends on our understanding of God: is this a God of wrath or a God of love?

We may also ask the question, Is the expression "reign of God" the only one by which the divine presence can be expressed? We may note some of its advantages right away. It is no mere concept, but points directly to the dynamic aspect of God. When taken to mean "kingdom," it allows us to dream of the wonderful result of the divine activity but without permitting us to identify this with any earthly realization, including the church itself. The other meaning, that of "reign," invites us to pray to the Lord, "Let your reign begin!"[36] Moreover, the two sayings of Jesus, about the imminence and the actualization of the reign, encourage the believer not to bewail any setbacks that are encountered, but to look, in the realities of this world, for partial actualizations of its presence.

We will discover, in the following chapters, the nature of the presence of God-in-action, which Jesus experienced: God takes the initiative in forgiving, without anything being required on the part of humans. As we anticipate this discussion, it is appropriate to show how Jesus portrayed the presence of God-at-work. We may describe this with two expressions: an urgent presence (seeking dialogue) and a mysterious presence.

---

[36] Here the author quotes a phrase from the Lord's Prayer in French that is typically rendered in English, "Thy kingdom come." I have translated the French using the term "reign" instead, which the context calls for.—Trans.

A Presence Seeking a Response

God always comes to us seeking a dialogue; he expects a response from us, that of welcoming his love. We must therefore "stay alert" so that we can seize the moment, the favorable *kairos*.

In his first announcement, Jesus declared that this *kairos* had been fulfilled (Mark 1:15). Hence,

> Beware, keep alert; for you do not know when the time will come. (Mark 13:33)

There is no sign that allows us to be ready for the encounter. Thus, when the Pharisees demanded from Jesus a sign from heaven,

> [12]he sighed deeply in his spirit and said, "Why does this generation ask for a sign? Truly I tell you, no sign will be given to this generation." (Mark 8:12)

> [54]He also said to the crowds, "When you see a cloud rising in the west, you immediately say, 'It is going to rain'; and so it happens. [55]And when you see the south wind blowing, you say, 'There will be scorching heat'; and it happens. [56]You hypocrites! You know how to interpret the appearance of earth and sky, but why do you not know how to interpret the present time?" (Luke 12:54–56)

The refrain comes constantly from the lips of Jesus:

> Keep awake therefore, for you know neither the day nor the hour. (Matt 25:13)

These warnings have to do particularly with the return of the Son of Man, but Jesus does not limit his teaching to the final Parousia; he envisions all the situations where God is present among people. The parable of the Sheep and the Goats provides sufficient evidence of this: we must act throughout life as if we recognized Jesus himself:

> Just as you did it to one of the least of these who are members of my family, you did it to me. (Matt 25:40)

Jesus is present in the "least of these" because God himself is present, with a presence that requires an effective response from us. His is the presence of a love that becomes pressing, that requires each of us to stir ourselves up to become truly open to what is happening.

Some of the parables give examples of urgent situations that the "children of light" need to seize by the horns in order to extricate themselves. One of these is the parable of the Shrewd Manager (Luke 16:1–8a). This story troubled the gospel tradition itself, as the additions that seek to give it a "more acceptable" sense testify. This parable was not told to teach about money;[37] rather, the lesson is that we need to know how to get moving in a crucial situation.

> Jesus said to the disciples, "There was a rich man who had a manager, and charges were brought to him that this man was squandering his property. [2]So he summoned him and said to him, 'What is this that I hear about you? Give me an accounting of your management, because you cannot be my manager any longer.' [3]Then the manager said to himself, 'What will I do, now that my master is taking the position away from me? I am not strong enough to dig, and I am ashamed to beg. [4]I have decided

---

[37] The successive additions have brought together recollections of Jesus talking about the love of money, stored up for its own sake; a saying of Jesus advising us to make friends for ourselves by using mammon so that they will receive us into heaven (16:9); and one about being found faithful so as not to be led astray by money (16:10–12). Finally, to cap off this diatribe against those with possessions, the terrible verdict is delivered: "You cannot serve God and wealth" (16:13).

what to do so that, when I am dismissed as manager, people may welcome me into their homes.' [5]So, summoning his master's debtors one by one, he asked the first, 'How much do you owe my master?' [6]He answered, 'A hundred jugs of olive oil.' He said to him, 'Take your bill, sit down quickly, and make it fifty.' [7]Then he asked another, 'And how much do you owe?' He replied, 'A hundred containers of wheat.' He said to him, 'Take your bill and make it eighty.' [8]And his master commended the dishonest manager because he had acted shrewdly; for the children of this age are more shrewd in dealing with their own generation than are the children of light. (Luke 16:1–8)

Familiar as we are today with cases of embezzlement, we are astonished when we see Jesus use such an example. How can the master praise this man who has just defrauded him? But what is praiseworthy in the story is not the dishonesty of the manager, but rather his resourcefulness, as the conclusion emphasizes: the "children of light" are less resourceful than those of the world. But they are the ones who must secure the future that the reign of God is inaugurating.

One question, however, remains unanswered: who is the "master" who praises the manager? A good theory is often proposed: Luke's style seems to indicate that, at an early stage, the "lord" of v. 8 indicated Jesus himself. The "Lord" sang the praises of the manager. In any event, the parable's own teaching can be summarized this way: "You are astonished! But take the lesson to heart: you need to become able to deal with the difficult situation you are in. Otherwise, you will be left out of the reign of God." Now that's a call to know how to get out of a tight spot, and to become radically engaged.

A Mysterious Presence

Jesus announced that God was at work and was expecting a warm welcome. We must loyally acknowledge, however, that he did not meet with success, other than the momentary enthusiasm of the crowds. Matthew expressed this well by showing that after the initial success of his preaching, Jesus described the results of his ministry through the story of the seeds: the parable of the Sower recounts the history of Jesus.

In this story Jesus tells how what seemed like a futile scattering of seed nevertheless bore fruit in the end.[38] We certainly do not need to imagine that the interpretation proposed in Matthew is more valuable or historic than those of the other two Synoptic Gospels, but fortunately it does show how Jesus faced a lack of success. This shows us that it is important to situate any setbacks within the grand design of God the Father, who, despite everything, is bringing about success, in a manner that we call "mysterious."

We may number among the authentic teachings of Jesus his concern for the "Messianic secret," at whose core lies the sense of "mystery," of something beyond the visible that depends on a being unknown to the greater part of humanity. Jesus told stories that showed the surprising future of the word of God:

> [30]With what can we compare the kingdom of God, or what parable will we use for it? [31]It is like a mustard seed, which, when sown upon the ground, is the smallest of all the seeds on earth; [32]yet when it is sown it grows up and becomes the greatest of all shrubs, and puts forth large branches, so that the birds of the air can make nests in its shade. (Mark 4:30–32)

The parables of the Hidden Treasure and the Pearl of Great Price express the mysterious aspect of the reign of God

The story of a man who unabashedly gets rich by accidentally discovering a hidden treasure is part of the human

---

[38]Matt 13:3–9 and pars. This interpretation is developed in my *Études d'évangile* (Paris: Seuil, 1965), 292–301.

heritage; such stories were told just as freely in the Hellenistic universe as in the Jewish world. Jesus makes it his own and adds a second, analogous story, which is different in that the hero is no longer a lucky person but someone who is seeking something rare. I don't know whether a similar story is to be found in folklore, but as a metaphor it is applicable to all of human experience: we are always looking for someone or for something, someone to love or something that will make us rich. Two kinds of people are thus depicted, to show that everyone is included.

> The kingdom of heaven is like treasure hidden in a field, which someone found and hid; then in his joy he goes and sells all that he has and buys that field.

> Again, the kingdom of heaven is like a merchant in search of fine pearls; on finding one pearl of great value, he went and sold all that he had and bought it. (Matt 13:44–46)

Jesus' biblical inheritance shines through the human background of these stories; the themes of meeting and discovery are those characteristically applied to Wisdom: it is a treasure,[39] a pearl.[40] We must search for Wisdom in order to find it.[41]

We should not interpret these two parables as allegories and look for what each separate element means, as by saying, for example, that the treasure and the pearl represent Christ.[42] These are rather stories told whose characters might be called "players": the reign of heaven; the discoverer of the treasure or

---

[39] Prov 2:4; 8:18.

[40] Prov 3:15; 8:11; Job 28:18.

[41] Prov 1:20–28; Wis 6:12–19.

[42] Allegory is present elsewhere, for example, in the interpretation of the parable of the Sower (Matt 13:18–23) and that of the parable of the Tares (Matt 13:36–43), where each element of the parable is "allegorized."

of the pearl. The worker and the merchant *find*, one by chance and the other at the end of a long search. The worker and the merchant *sell* their goods and buy the field or the pearl. If they find, it's because something has been hidden, something of great value, the treasure or the pearl. What was hidden certainly was very valuable, because they sell everything in order to buy it.

The listener is expected to understand that when faced with a unique reality, the proper response is to give up everything in order to obtain it. This is not to embrace a sort of voluntary poverty (this would be to allegorize), but rather to be in a position to engage oneself totally and joyfully with something so valuable. The message of the story is indicated in its introduction: it has to do with the reign of God, that is, with God in the process of acting to establish his reign. Knowing that this is what God is doing, when I meet him, I respond with a joy that leads me to give everything. We will explore this more in chapter 3, where we will discuss the obstacles to welcoming the reign of God.

The old and the new

Jesus' contemporaries wanted to add to the law many customs that had hardly anything to do with it. He responded to them incisively with a saying that tolerated no compromise:

> No one puts new wine into old wineskins; otherwise, the wine will burst the skins, and the wine is lost, and so are the skins; but one puts new wine into new wineskins. (Mark 2:22 and pars., NRSV, var.)

This radical saying is preceded in the entire Synoptic tradition by another saying, which is no less radical, about the incompatibility between the new and the old:

> No one sews a piece of unshrunk cloth on an old cloak; otherwise, the patch pulls away from it, the new from the old, and a worse tear is made. (Mark 2:21 and pars.)

In hearing these parables some might have thought about how to take care of their wine, and others about mending their clothes, but Jesus' adversaries especially heard the prophet crying out his opposition, like another Jeremiah: we must choose definitively between the old and the new.

But what is the "old," and what is the "new"? One thing is certain: "old" cannot be the covenant that God made with Israel. It would be absurd to cut the gospel off from its roots, the First Testament. This is what John explains in the Cana episode: the new wine was not created out of nothing; it came from the water in the stone jars, which were themselves used in the Jewish purification ritual. And this water was previously the water of the original creation. The original occasion of these sayings is uncertain, but each of the Synoptic evangelists has situated them in a similar context, suggesting that they are in response to the practice of devotional fasting, a supererogatory practice not sanctioned in the law.

As for the "new," the context of the gospel as a whole suggests that it is the teaching of Jesus, or his experience of newness, that coincided with his experience of God's unrivaled reign.

By Way of Conclusion

At the end of this brief inquiry into the Synoptic tradition, we can say one thing for certain: Jesus had the experience that God was offering something absolutely new to Israel and to the world, something foreseen long ago by the prophets and now ready to happen. This experience was so strong that he devoted his whole life to communicating it: "God is coming!"

In doing this, he appeared to be conscious of fulfilling a mission that had been entrusted to him, since he had been given power from on high to defeat the one who opposed God's design and tormented men. In the texts that we have cited,

Jesus does not offer any formulas for what this new thing might be. Since he was speaking to his fellow Jews, his words would naturally have evoked their own timeless hopes. But they also spoke to the immediate, existential present, and not the end of the world. We have not wanted to be more explicit here, leaving this to the other chapters of this book. However, one thing is for sure: this man raises a question. Who can this man be, in whom and by whom God shows himself to be present? The Fourth Gospel offers an answer. Let's hear what it has to say.

ACCORDING TO THE GOSPEL OF JOHN

Certain critics would hold that we cannot pursue our investigation any further. Any supplemental information could only come from sources other than those that can properly be considered "historical." Those who would insist on such a rigorous approach certainly demonstrate their integrity as historians. But does this really do justice to all of the data? Over the past twenty years or so, exegetes have come to understand that we cannot appreciate all the riches of a text's meaning by reading it alone. They have appreciated the value of *Wirkungsgeschichte,* that is, the discipline of seeing how the meaning of a text is illuminated by its subsequent interpretations. The recent commentary on Matthew by U. Luz[43] shows clearly the contribution this method can make.

Nevertheless, the proper objective of exegetical inquiry is not to pursue this task the whole length of the tradition. The exegete's responsibility is to take the four gospels into account. The historico-critical method excludes the Fourth Gospel on principle, since it is obviously an interpretation of the life of

---

[43] Ulrich Luz, *Das Evangelium nach Matthäus,* 4 vols. Evangelish-Katholischer Kommentar zum Neuen Testament (Vluyn: Neukirchener, 1985–1999).

Jesus. As was the custom with historians in antiquity, it puts words in Jesus' mouth, and as a result we cannot identify these words with his *ipsissima verba*. But if we are seeking to draw a portrait of Jesus, are we required on this basis to ignore John's interpretation of him?

Living with the memory of Jesus of Nazareth and his whole life story, this evangelist was able to penetrate in depth the meaning and the motivation of his behavior. He sought to express this in terms adapted to his time. The early church fully acknowledged this work and proclaimed its authenticity. That is why I believe we cannot speak of the experience of Jesus according to the gospel without examining the Johannine interpretation of it. This is, at least, my understanding of exegesis.

G. Soares-Prabhu, who is doing exegesis from an Indian perspective in response to the Third World's cry for a better life, has the same understanding. He once said to me,

> I'm not looking for the "Jesus of history" as unearthed by historical criticism. Nor am I looking for the "Christ of faith" presented to us in the dogmatic formulas of the churches. The object of my inquiry is what might be called the "Jesus of faith," that is, the One who is presented to us in the confessional history of the New Testament, which may not line up exactly with his critical history. The Jesus of faith is the Jesus of history as he was known in the experience of his faithful disciples.[44]

John Transposes the Expression basilea tou theou

By contrast with its frequency in the Synoptic tradition, the expression *basilea tou theou* appears in John in only two

---

[44] Cf. Michael A. Amaladoss and George M. Soares-Prabhu, *Wir werden bei ihm wohnen. Das Johannesevangelium in indischer Deutung* (Freiburg im Breisgau: Herder, 1984).

places, in the dialogue that Jesus has with Nicodemus (John 3:3, 5). There it is a matter of "entering into [or seeing] the kingdom of God." In this passage, the term signifies not the "reign [that is] coming," but the "kingdom" into which one enters, that is, "eternal life." What, then, is the Johannine equivalent of *basilea tou theou* in the sense of the "reign of God?"

Some believe that John translates the expression "reign of God" by the term "life," which is indeed of primary importance in his gospel. Whether or not accompanied by the adjective "eternal," it designates both the communion that the believer will ultimately enjoy with God and the real communion one already has with God in this world. But while it does evoke one result of the activity of God, it does not describe that activity itself.

Another term in this gospel, "light," is often identified with God himself, with the Logos, with Jesus of Nazareth. It overcomes the darkness when it comes into the world; it illuminates every person; it demands to be engaged.[45] Nevertheless, even though the metaphor describes very well the divine action of the Logos, or of Jesus, it does not imply an intrinsic connection with the Father who sent him.

In my view, while the coming of the reign of God constitutes the central message of the Synoptics, the Johannine text is organized around the idea of the "one sent from the Father." This formula retains the role of the "Messiah," who, in the Synoptics, is more of a question than an answer. It also preserves the essence of the famous saying of Jesus that he was known by the Father and that he alone knew the Father. This so-called Johannine logion[46] is just a glimmer in the Synoptics; in John, it becomes a recurrent theme.

---

[45] Skim my *Lecture de l'évangile selon Jean* (4 vols.; Paris: Seuil, 1988–1996), 1:84–100, 2:261–64.

[46] Luke 10:21–22 = Matt 11:25–27.

Jesus always considers himself the "one sent from the Father,"[47] which does not mean a delegate or an ambassador, despite certain unfortunate translations that misrepresent the exact nature of the relationship of the Son to his Father. For example, John 5:36 is often translated, "I have a testimony, which is greater than that of John: the works that the Father has given me to accomplish,"[48] as if Jesus had received an order to accomplish this or that work. The passage should really be translated:

> The works that my Father has given to me, that I might bring them to completion, these very works that I do bear witness on my behalf that the Father has sent me. (John 5:36, author's translation)

The Father gave Jesus these works, and he is going to bring them to completion. These works are the works of the Father; they are also the works of the Son, indivisibly.[49] The Father did not simply turn over his works, as to an executor; he wanted them to be truly his own. The Son thus gives tangible form to the divine power of salvation. The invisible takes on a human face.

The Mystery of "Two and One"

To express this mystery, the evangelist makes two successive affirmations that may appear to contradict one another,

---

[47] John 4:34; 5:23–24, 36ff; 6:29, 38, 44–45; 7:16, 33; 8:16, 18, 29, 42; 9:4; 11:42; 12:44–45; 14:24; 15:21; 17:3, 8, 18, 21, 25; 20:21.

[48] *TOB.*

[49] A. Vanhoye masterfully disclosed this nuance, which is of considerable theological significance, in *Recherches de science religieuse* 48 (1960): 377–419. The original Greek text, *ta erga ha dedōken moi ho patēr hina teleiōsō auta,* requires that it be a matter not of works *to* accomplish, but of "works that the Father has given me *so that* I might bring them to completion."

but that maintain the two aspects under which a symbolic reality is being presented; it *is and is not* the reality itself. John uses the formula "two and one."

His prologue thus begins by announcing, "The Word was with God" (1:1a). "With God" means that they are *two.* But then, right afterward, he says that "the Word *was* God" (1:1b). The Word and God are therefore *one.* Jesus, who is the Word incarnate, will be presented in the course of this gospel as both distinct from the Father and as one with the Father.

In seeking to understand this mystery, it is helpful to remind ourselves that it expresses an authentic biblical mysticism, as opposed to a mysticism that would dream of fusion with the divine. Al-Hallaj, the tenth-century Muslim mystic, cried out wonderfully in one of his poems,

> Between you and me there is an *it's me* that torments me.
> Oh, by your *it's me,* remove my *it's me* from between *we two.*

The desire expressed here ends in the suppression, through fusion, of one of the two parties in the relationship. It must not happen this way according to biblical revelation: the *two* in the relationship become *one* without ceasing to be *two,* thanks to the *communion* that draws them together. Such is the mystery of the covenant.

Before proclaiming that Jesus and the Father are *one,* John's prologue begins by affirming that they are *two:*

> No one has ever seen God;
> The only-begotten Son, God who is in the bosom of the
>   Father,
> He has made him known. (John 1:18, author's translation)

The incarnate Word is the one who makes God known. He is God's "Sent One," constituting with God an "other" than himself. Nevertheless, he is fully conscious of his indefectible union with the Father, in the form of a presence:

> The one who sent me is with me;
> he has not left me alone,
> for I always do what is pleasing to him. (John 8:29)

When his disciples were going to be scattered one from another, leaving him alone, Jesus affirmed,

> Yet I am not alone. (John 16:32)

This is sufficient to discredit, if necessary, the unfortunate interpretation sometimes given to Jesus' cry from the cross, *"Eloi, Eloi lema sabachthani?"*[50] When the time came to face death on the cross, Jesus ascended to glory. "He is going back to the One who sent him" (John 7:33; 16:5).

But even as Jesus attested to his profound communion with the Father, he affirmed just as clearly:

> The Father is greater than I. (John 14:28)

This affirmation has troubled the Christian tradition to the extent that it has been isolated from its context. Jesus clearly understands himself here as the "One who was sent," who is not greater than the One who sent him (cf. John 13:16). And we should add to this explanation the observation that there is a literary connection between this affirmation and the theme of the disciples' joy: Jesus' return to his Father opens the way to the Father for them definitively.[51]

Because he and the Father are distinct beings, Jesus could appropriately appeal, in his controversies with the Jews, to the testimony of his Father. His adversaries consequently demanded, "Where is your Father?" (John 8:19). This produced an awkward situation, because the Father is visible only to the

---

[50] I have attempted to show what this cry means in the Synoptics in *Face à la mort, Jésus et Paul* (Paris: Seuil, 1979), 149–67.

[51] I have explored this connection in my *Lecture de l'évangile selon Jean*, 3:137–39.

eyes of faith. In fact, it was an impossible situation, even for the
disciples, who themselves asked, in the person of Philip: "Lord,
show us the Father, and we will be satisfied" (John 14:8). But it
is a good situation for those who, by faith, recognize the perfect
transparency of the Father and the Son:

> Jesus said to him, "Have I been with you all this time, Philip,
> and you still do not know me? Whoever has seen me has seen
> the Father." (John 14:9)

The mystery of the presence of the incarnate Word only
discloses itself to faith. This disclosure does not consist in a
revelation of the exact nature of the Son's union with the
Father, but rather in an understanding that the activity of the
Son is identical with that of the Father. This is what Jesus affirmed when he used the metaphor of the shepherd and his
sheep. In the face of his adversaries' disbelief, Jesus insisted:

> No one will snatch them out of my hand. My Father who has
> given them to me is greater than all, and no one can snatch
> them out of the Father's hand. The Father and I are one [*hen*].
> (John 10:28–30, NRSV, marg.)

The text is only envisioning a unity of action, as the neuter *hen*
suggests, so that it might be translated, "My Father and I are
only doing one thing," although Jesus does give us a glimpse of
a more profound union, leading the reader to recall the statement in the prologue that the Word was God. The later tradition appealed to this text to establish the unity of the divine
substance between Father and Son. It justified its interpretation through a variant reading of v. 29, retained by the Vulgate:
"What the Father has given me"—understood to mean the divine nature—"is greater than all." But John maintains the distinction of the persons without thereby elaborating a theology
of "two natures." In John's understanding, Jesus was fully conscious of acting in communion, not fusion, with the Father.

This gives us an insight into what the experience of Jesus was according to the Fourth Gospel: God was in the depths of his being; his action was that of the Father.

The Action of the Son Is the Action of the Father

The key to the action of the Son is found in the discourse that follows the healing of the sick man at Bethsaida (John 5). Jesus has just said, "My Father is still working, and I also am working," leading the Jews to want to kill him for making himself "equal to God" (5:17–18). Their accusation reveals the ambiguity of Jesus' language: would he be independent of God, and even a second God? But in the discourse that follows, Jesus reaffirms the monotheism that defines Judaism and Christianity. This discourse also unveils the mystery of the Son, in whom the absolute of a dependency lived out within a relationship of love proves to be of inconceivable dignity.

These words show clearly that the Father is not a God immobilized in eternity, but the One who acts. The One who is the source of Jesus' action does not give him works to do, but empowers him to act. God "personalizes" his Son, giving him everything he is: life, light, and everything he does.

The Action of the Believer Must Be the Action of the Son

If Jesus is the one who makes the face of the Father personally present, it follows that the mysterious relationship that unites him to the Father is the prototype of the relationship that unites the believer to Christ:

> Just as [*kathos*] the living Father sent me, and I live because
> of the Father,
> so [*kai*] whoever eats me will live because of me.
> Those who eat my flesh and drink my blood abide in me, and
> I in them. (John 6:57, 56)

The reciprocal relationship that is established between the Son and the believer is founded on and animated by the relationship that unites the Father and the Son.[52] The conjunction *kathos* followed by *kai* does not simply introduce a comparison between two realities; its actual purpose is to describe an intrinsic connection between two existing relationships that are analogous to one another. The relationship between the Father and the Son is the foundational model. Every action and all life that originates in the living Father can only continue to exist in relationship with him, whether in the Son or in the believer. This is the meaning of the "abiding" that will henceforth express the relationship between the Father and the Son, and the relationship between the Son and the believer.

John's perspective is seen in the way that it is almost impossible to speak of the Father except in relationship with Jesus, his Son. The Father exists, he acts, but he does not have an "individuality" that can be juxtaposed with that of Jesus. Nevertheless, the Father and the Son cannot be confused with one another. They are *two* even as they are *one*. This is a further aspect of the paradox of their relationship.

Conclusion

According to the Synoptic tradition, Jesus had the experience of God, who triumphed over the Adversary through him. His action relied on God; he was the active presence of God. He needed to fulfill this unique and indispensable role in order for the reign of God to be realized. The Fourth Gospel invites us to interiorize the relationship between Jesus and God from the perspective of immanence. This is the significance of the *one* that the *two beings* are: one of them is in the other.

---

[52] I have taken up this subject in my *Lecture de l'évangile selon Jean*.

This Johannine interpretation does not invalidate the Synoptic presentation. Rather, it shows the reader how the revelation concerning the experience of Jesus unfolded. It was appropriate (we could even say necessary) to have begun with language that expressed his relationship with God as that of a counterpart. In other words, in this first understanding they are *two beings, face to face.*

Can we not generalize and observe that this paradox expresses the mystery of God, who is at the same time both transcendent and immanent? We typically represent these two characteristics spatially: transcendence becomes "otherness" and immanence becomes "interiority." But this creates the risk of either making God an idol at our disposal, or else falling into a pantheism that knows nothing of transcendence.

SYNOPSIS

The fundamental experience of Jesus has a double aspect. It was rooted in the religious experience of Israel and represented a highly developed expression of it. The people of Israel had been chosen by a Being who entered into an eternal covenant with them. Despite their continual infidelities, they came to understand that God's fidelity did not depend on their own, because God is a God of forgiveness. God would bring to completion the covenant he had made with them.

But the experience of Jesus must also be called "original" at the same time. We can see that God's activity was concentrated on Jesus of Nazareth, given the radical way in which he triumphed over the Adversary. Was he not, even more than the prophets, a privileged instrument of God?

While the Synoptic tradition shows great restraint in not wanting to make Jesus another God, the Beloved Disciple penetrated into the mystery of this surprising man and dared to claim that he was God (which Jesus himself did not do).

Specifically, he is God's Son, both by his own origin and by his faithfulness unto death. Indeed, he is one with God himself. In other words, John understood Jesus as the covenant personified. Did Jesus himself realize this? John does not show us a being who proclaimed himself to be God, but he makes it clear that anyone should be able to recognize him as such. Jesus thus becomes the prototype of a person united to God through the covenant, which found its accomplishment in him.

Chapter 2

Jesus in Relation to Jewish Tradition

ACCORDING TO THE SYNOPTIC TRADITION

Jesus was not alone. Infused with the presence of God, who even then was reigning over his people, Jesus captivated some of his contemporaries, but he quickly came into conflict with the religious establishment, which reproached him for not observing the venerable traditions handed down from their ancestors. This was the main reason for his condemnation.

The situation in which Jesus found himself is typical of those who are not content to follow the customs of their time. Such is the lot of reformers, of mystics, of charismatics. This often results in "sects," which sometimes remain marginal, but which sometimes also expand into established communities, such as religions like Christianity or Islam, or religious orders, to speak only of institutions that are recognized today. On a more general level, the same conflict can be recognized in adolescents who take a stand in opposition to their parents, or to what we might call the "received tradition!"

Jesus himself was not afraid to challenge noble habits such as the Sabbath rest and the purity regulations, disturbing the customs of his time without hesitation. From his behavior and the violent reactions of his contemporaries, many have concluded that Jesus was opposed to the Jewish law. This has led to a caricature of both the Jews and Jesus, and to the view that the good news was meant to supplant the Jewish law. But this understanding is not truly based on the data in the gospels. There has also been no shortage of interpreters who have identified the teaching of Jesus with a new law, an extension of the Jewish Torah. It is important, therefore, to examine the texts themselves and get back to the thought of Jesus, to the greatest extent possible. Let us first briefly review the place of the Torah in Jewish life, so that we can appreciate the preeminent role that tradition played in it.

The Torah and the Halakah

The term "Torah" comes from the root *yarah*, which means "to indicate a direction," "to teach," "to instruct." When the Septuagint translated this Hebrew term with the word *nomos*, it emphasized its legal aspect, to the detriment of its revelatory one. Originally, the term designated a specific commandment. Eventually, the collected Torah became part of the Book of the Covenant. The Torah only exists in relationship with the covenant. It therefore finds its fullest meaning only when it is the people's response to God making his will known to them. There is a danger that the Torah will lead to a blind obedience if it is isolated from the covenant. If the Decalogue[1] does not lead to a dialogue, it's nothing more than a catalogue.

With the end of the exile, a hardening occurred that turned the law into a protective hedge around the community.

---

[1] Exod 20:1–17; Deut 5:6–21.

In this context, around 500 B.C.E., the Pentateuch was created by putting legal texts together with some narratives. The Torah as we know it today is the product of the Babylonian Diaspora. It was the source of most of what would come to be known as Judaism, whose chief exponent was Ezra (c. 398 B.C.E.). This Judaism was intensified by the Maccabean crisis of around 175 B.C.E., and ultimately, with the monastery at Qumran and the agitation of the Zealots, the law was absolutized. As a result, any critique of the law or of the cult became an attack on the Jewish faith itself. When Wisdom was identified with the Torah,[2] the Torah, with its 613 commandments, came to dominate Jewish existence. It became the sole way of understanding creation and salvation, to the point where it was believed that God himself "consulted" the Torah.

Fortunately, a counterbalancing influence emerged, the halakah.

> In the Pharisees' understanding, the Torah was composed, on the one hand, of the divine revelation contained in the five books of Moses, which was complemented and actualized by the teaching of the 'Law' and the 'Writings'—this was the written Torah—and on the other hand, of the unwritten tradition, the oral Torah, which was also received by Moses on Mount Sinai and passed on to Joshua and then to his successors, just as the written Torah had been.[3]

One therefore had to be acquainted with the "oral tradition," which was called the *halakah,* a term derived from the root *halak,* "to go, to walk," walking being an ancient biblical metaphor for human behavior in all of one's existence.[4] In general

---

[2] Sir 1, 24.

[3] Pierre Lenhardt and Matthieu Collin, *La Torah orale des pharisiens. Textes de la Tradition d'Israël, Cahiers Évangile* 73, supplement (Cerf, 1990), 109. Cf. *DNT,* 77–79.

[4] Lev 26:3; Deut 11:22.

terms, halakah designates that which concerns the practice of
the law. The word can refer to a particular norm or the sum total
of the norms according to which Jewish existence should be con-
ducted. Thus it can indicate the entire legal domain. We should
not imply that everything depended on the halakah, but it does
point to the existence of an oral tradition that "preceded, accomplished and contained the written tradition it transmitted, whose
unity it manifested; this oral tradition could sometimes sidestep,
supersede or uproot the written Torah itself."[5]

Different interpretations all had to be mentioned, because
the meaning of the Torah, Jewish authors said, would only be
made clear at the end of time.[6] What mattered was not the system, but the commentary that was offered as all of the interpretations were listed.

Jesus observed the law, both by revealing its deepest
meaning and by situating it in relationship with his personal
experience of God's love. We may therefore assert that the conflict between Jesus and his contemporaries was not so much
about the law itself as about how it should be interpreted. It
was a conflict between Jewish tradition, which had been codified under the aegis of Moses, and Jesus, who lived in direct
relationship with God.

Jesus and Jewish Tradition

Absence of interest in the law as such

The term *nomos,* indicating the Jewish law, is not found
in Mark and occurs only rarely in Q;[7] it is sometimes found in

---

[5] Lenhardt and Collin, *La Torah orale,* 107–8.

[6] P. Hoffman, 82, quotes G. Scholem (1970) and adds a comment about the Christian concept of tradition, which tolerates
no error.

[7] Luke 16:17.

controversy accounts in Matthew and Luke.[8] On the other hand, it is often combined with *prophetai* to indicate the whole Bible, "the law and the prophets."[9] As for the terms *nomos* and *entolai* meaning commandments or particular precepts, they are used only in Mark.[10]

When Jesus spoke of the law with "the prophets," he was situating it within the Bible as a whole. Thus, when asked by a lawyer what the greatest commandment in the law was, Jesus cited the commandments to love God and neighbor, and concluded: "On these two commandments hang all the law and the prophets" (Matt 22:40). The conclusion is inescapable: Jesus appears to have had no interest in the law as such.

On the threshold of the reign of God

However, Jesus situated himself in relation to John the Baptist in such a way as to mark off two periods: the time when the reign of God is proclaimed, and the time beforehand. John the Baptist is situated on the threshold of the reign of God:

> Among those born of women no one is greater than John; yet the least according to the kingdom of God is greater than he.[11] (Luke 7:28, NRSV, var.)

John does not yet belong to the kingdom of God that Jesus has announced. This announcement demarcated a new period, in

---

[8] Matt 12:5; 15:6; 22:36; 23:23; Luke 10:26.

[9] Matt 5:17; 7:12; 11:13; 22:40 = Luke 16:16; 24:44.

[10] Mark 7:8–9; 10:5, 19; 12:28, 31.

[11] The preposition *en* followed by a substantive indicating a person can signify "in the eyes of," "in the judgment of," or "for" (1 Cor 4:11); cf. Anatole Bailly, Louis Séchan, and Pierre Chantraine, *Dictionnaire grec-français* (26th ed.; Paris: Hachette, 1950), s.v. "*en.*" In this case, "reign of heaven" is equivalent to "God-who-reigns"; it is "according to" the judgment of God that one is called "small" or "great."

which the Torah continues to express the will of God, but in which it must be understood in a new way, in light of its relationship to the reign of God, which is the ultimate criterion of Christian action.

The same affirmation of two successive periods is present in an important saying whose original wording is difficult to determine:[12]

> From the days of John the Baptist until now the kingdom of heaven has suffered violence (*biazetai*), and the violent (*biastai*) take it by force. (Matt 11:12)

Luke proposes another interpretation of Jesus' saying:

> The law and the prophets were in effect until John came; since then the good news of the kingdom of God is proclaimed (*euangelizetai*), and everyone tries to enter it by force (*eis auten biazetai*). (Luke 16:16)

According to Matthew, the reign of God is the victim (the term *biazetai* is taken in a passive sense), and the violent (the term *biastai* is taken in a pejorative sense) are those who prevent people from entering it. According to Luke, the reign of God is the object of the good news, and those who strive to enter it do so with violence (*biazetai* is taken in a positive sense). But whichever sense we choose, we can recognize the existence of two periods, each with a different basis of action: the time of the law and the time of the reign of God.

One fact is unavoidable: the good news of the reign unleashes violence, as other sayings of Jesus make clear.

---

[12]Merklein, 71–90, proposes that the saying may have read this way in Q:

> The Law and the prophets were until John;
> from this moment on the Reign of God arrives with violence,
> and the violent seize it.

> Do you think that I have come to bring peace to the earth? No,
> I tell you, but rather division! (Luke 12:51 = Matt 10:34)

And listen to what Jesus said on another occasion:

> [21]Another of his disciples said to him, "Lord, first let me go and
> bury my father." [22]But Jesus said to him, "Follow me, and let
> the dead bury their own dead." (Matt 8:21–22)

By giving this incisive response, Jesus was not disparaging the
fourth commandment in any way, but he was making it give
way before another calling: to follow him and become part of
spreading the good news. Jesus was thus subordinating a precept of the law to the imperative of the reign of God. The reign
is a new thing, and whoever allows himself to be grasped by it
will have to make a similar choice. Jesus does not criticize the
Torah; he only situates it in relation to the experience of God-
who-is-reigning.

The law is still in effect

But there is a paradox: right after the saying that "the law
and the prophets were in effect until John came," Luke relates
a second saying that proclaims that the law is still in effect:

> It is easier for heaven and earth to pass away, than for one
> stroke of a letter in the law to be dropped. (Luke 16:17)

This saying, which is certainly authentic, counterbalances the
affirmation of the preceding verse. If the whole law were swept
aside, would this not lead to the kind of libertinage the Jews
witnessed among the pagans? To counter this possible excess,
this saying insists on the enduring value of the law. In fact,
Jesus criticized the scribes and the Pharisees for having "ne-
glected the weightier matters of the law: justice and mercy and
faith" (Matt 23:23). Nevertheless, this saying does not distinguish what is essential from what is incidental; rather, it radi-
calizes the value of every element of the law.

In what sense? Let us seek to determine this by examining Matt 5:17–20, which offers, in v. 18, a parallel to Luke 16:17.

> [17]Do not think that I have come to abolish the law or the prophets; I have come not to abolish but to fulfill. [18]For truly I tell you, until heaven and earth pass away, not one letter, not one stroke of a letter, will pass from the law until all is accomplished (*genetai*). [19]Therefore (*oun*), whoever breaks one of the least of these commandments, and teaches others to do the same, will be called least in (*en //*) the kingdom of heaven; but whoever does them and teaches them will be called great in (*en //*) the kingdom of heaven. [20]For I tell you, unless your righteousness exceeds that of the scribes and Pharisees, you will never enter the kingdom of heaven. (Matt 5:17–20)

This grouping of sayings attributed to Jesus is so artificial that critics typically do not even try to justify its composition.[13] The first and last sayings (vv. 17, 20) are appropriate to serve as an introduction to the first section of the Sermon on the Mount, which concerns Jesus' position relative to the law (Matt 5:17–7:12). The verses these two sayings frame (vv. 18–19), on the other hand, raise several questions. Does the law remain in force until the end of time, even though Jesus himself appears often to have infringed it? Does the reign of heaven judge our conduct by how well we keep the law, even though it establishes a new era of moral conduct?

One response would be that these middle verses should be attributed to Christians who were concerned for keeping the law in force. But in that case, how could Matthew have attributed these words to Jesus? If he had, we would suspect him of having been the partisan of some extremist Jewish-Christian

---

[13]Daniel Marguerat, *Le jugement dans l'évangile de Matthieu*, 2d ed. (Geneva: Labor et Fides, 1995), 110–41, thinks that Matthew used the Q-saying found in Luke 16:17 and then strengthened his interpretation of it with the help of Mark 13:32.

sect. But he seems rather to have been more like certain Christians whom Paul talks about.[14]

We should therefore prefer a different explanation. Even though we must acknowledge that these sayings come from a "conservative" milieu, we can also imagine that Matthew understood them to refer not to the law in its classic sense but rather to a law newly interpreted by Jesus. And the interpretation is indeed radical: "The law and the prophets" consist in "do[ing] to others as you would have them do to you" (7:12). In this sense, the law is fulfilled in the reign of God.

Following Jesus

On two occasions, Jesus disclosed that we must now relate to him, rather than to the commandments. The first was when the rich young ruler asked him what he needed to "do to inherit eternal life."[15] In response, Jesus enumerated several commandments that were all prohibitions except the last, which had to do with respect for parents. It's surprising that love of God is never mentioned, and that love of neighbor only appears in Matthew's version (Matt 19:19), where the command to love one's neighbor as oneself and the command to honor father and mother are treated as one, which is something new. But the point of the story is otherwise:

> Come, follow me! (Matt 19:21)

What this man needed to do, in effect, was to welcome the reign of God by divesting himself of his riches (Mark 10:25).

---

[14] Paul Beauchamp suggests an interpretation that goes in this direction in *La loi de Dieu* (Paris: Seuil, 1999), 123–25.

[15] The pericope (Mark 10:17–23 = Matt 19:16–22 = Luke 18:18–23) has been studied in detail by N. Walter, "Zur Analyse von Mc 10:17–31," *Zeitschrift für die neutestamentiche Wissenschaft* 53 (1962): 206–18, to which H. Merklein refers in *Die Gottesherrschaft*, 96–100. See also Beauchamp, *La loi de Dieu*, 13–28.

From this we see that it is no longer sufficient to keep the commandments of the Torah; we must follow Jesus in order to enter the new era, the reign of God.

In another passage concerning the *entolai,*[16] Jesus responds to a scribe's question, "What is the greatest of all the commandments?" He expounds the Torah by giving a précis:

> [29]The first [commandment] is, "Hear, O Israel: the Lord our God, the Lord is one; [30]you shall love the Lord your God with all your heart, and with all your soul, and with all your mind, and with all your strength." [31]The second is this, "You shall love your neighbor as yourself." There is no other commandment greater than these. (Mark 12:29–31)

Matthew adds:

> [38]This is the greatest and first commandment. [39]And a second is like it: "You shall love your neighbor as yourself." [40]On these two commandments hang all the law and the prophets. (Matt 22:38–40)

The scribe seeks to answer "wisely" by repeating the words of Jesus, who, for his part, tells him he is "not far from the kingdom of God" (Mark 12:34). He does not tell him that he lacks something, because the obstacle for him is not money, but the failure to understand the newness of what Jesus is bringing. Nevertheless it is thus implicitly announced that the reign of God awaits the scribe, at the end of an inquiry that must not content itself with establishing a hierarchy of commandments; rather, it must welcome the ultimate revelation in the person of Jesus.

Was Jesus faithful to the Torah?

There is one more objection to Jesus' faithfulness to the Torah. How are we to explain his frequent transgression of the

---

[16]Mark 12:28–34. Cf. Merklein, 100–107.

Sabbath rest? This was, according to the gospel writers, one of the reasons why he was condemned to death.[17] Granted, but the halakah authorized certain kinds of work on the Sabbath when it was a matter of urgency. Jesus reminded his detractors of this:[18]

> Does not each of you on the sabbath untie his ox or his donkey from the manger, and lead it away to give it water? (Luke 13:15)

Jesus meets the Jews on their own ground and appeals to a common practice authorized by the halakah. However, he locates the motivation on a much higher plane: to save life or to kill?[19] He is inspired by his fundamental experience: God is present, reigning.

Did Jesus transgress the laws of purity that determined the conditions of access to the sacred zone that a holy God had reserved for himself in the midst of a profane world?[20] Jesus certainly was not afraid to touch a leper or women who were in a state of ritual impurity, nor to sit at table with sinners. But should we conclude from this that Jesus was urging his followers to liberate themselves from the ceremonial laws of the Torah? This would be to overlook certain of his sayings that presuppose the validity of these prescriptions:

> [23]So when you are offering your gift at the altar, if you remember that your brother or sister has something against you, [24]leave your gift there before the altar and go; first be

---

[17]Mark 3:6. John does not limit himself to this one reason; he adds explicitly that Jesus called himself the "Son of God" (John 5:18).

[18]Cf. Matt 12:11–12; Luke 14:5.

[19]Cf. Beauchamp, *La loi de Dieu,* 171–90, where considerations relating to the Sabbath are pursued.

[20]Exod 19:10; Lev 11–16; Num 6:3. Cf. *DNT,* 460–61.

reconciled to your brother or sister, and then come and offer your gift. (Matt 5:23–24)

Another saying of Jesus seems to generalize his thinking on this matter. He said, in response to the Pharisees' criticism of his disciples for "eating with defiled hands":

There is nothing outside a person that by going in can defile, but the things that come out are what defile. (Mark 7:15)

This saying has often been interpreted as a criticism of the Torah. But this is incorrect;[21] even though Jesus was clearly disputing with the Pharisees over the custom of washing one's hands before meals, he was doing this not to abolish the Torah, but rather to situate this halakah in the overall context of hearing the word of God.

Such was the eschatological experience of the one who came to announce that the reign of God was henceforth present. It was no longer sufficient to appeal to the law to justify the validity of cultural practices; these had to be judged by reference to the love of God, which alone could give human action its ultimate meaning. It was out of love that Jesus made contacts that were ritually forbidden and sometimes found it expedient to break the Sabbath.[22]

The principle of action

By announcing that the reign of God was present, Jesus offered a new principle of action, one that did not abolish the

---

[21] Merklein has shown this clearly in the published version of his dissertation, *Jesu Botschaft von der Gottesherrschaft: Eine Skizze* (3d ed.; Stuttgart: Katholisches Bibelwerk, 1989), 96–101.

[22] In addition to Merklein, see D. Marguerat, who has given an excellent presentation on "Jesus and the Law" in *La mémoire et le temps: Mélanges offerts à Pierre Bonnard* (Geneva: Labor et Fides, 1991), 55–74.

Torah but rather revealed its meaning. A complicating factor is that some Christians, even though they were no longer trying to find salvation through the Torah, seemed to want to maintain a law of Jesus that was a homogeneous extension of the Jewish law.

We can thus detect a special concern for "doing" in the First Gospel, which sometimes comes out as a polemic against "legalists." But we do not need to conclude from this that Matthew believed in salvation by works. A Protestant brother has healthily engaged both Paul and Matthew and has concluded that the First Gospel is an "indispensable corrective to the Pauline gospel" because it shows how the commandments beneficially point beyond themselves: "The gift creates a responsibility that Matthew decodes in terms of brotherly love."[23] Matthew is therefore faithful to what Jesus proclaimed.

Jesus Takes a Stand

According to Matthew, Jesus demonstrated his radical attitude toward the Torah by means of the well-known "antitheses," which contrast his sayings with the formulations of Jewish tradition.

[21]You have heard that it was said to those of ancient times, *"You shall not murder"* and	[22]But I say to you that *if you are angry with a brother or sister,*
"whoever murders will be liable to judgment."	you will be liable to judgment. (Matt 5:21–22, italics added)

Jesus is not speaking here of the Torah as such, but with regard to the Torah as interpreted by the tradition. Jesus responds to this tradition by declaring the meaning of the Torah that he

---

[23]Marguerat, *Le Jugement,* 235.

knows from experience, as "one having authority, and not as their scribes" (Matt 7:29).

According to E. Lohse, this schema corresponds to that of a rabbinic dispute:[24] the phrases "have heard"[25] and "say" are technical terms by which the rabbis designated the acts of understanding and interpreting. Faced with a text of Scripture, they asked, "Should I understand it this way?" and then proposed an interpretation.[26] Thus, Jesus in Matthew would have been proceeding as follows: to an initial proposition (an interpretation of the law), one of his own sayings would have been opposed ("but I say to you . . .").

According to H. Merklein,[27] however, this way of looking at the antitheses does not respect their syntax. While "you have heard" uses the plural "you" of dialogue, the citation from the Torah is introduced objectively with an "it" ("it was said"). This has important consequences. The Pharisaic thesis proposes not a halakah, but the text of the Torah itself. Jesus thus opposes his living word even to that of the Torah, when it is read as an immutable written code. His experience of God led him to rediscover in the Torah a living text.

By examining three antitheses, considered as "primary" because they are not found in the other Synoptic Gospels, we will discover that in his critique, Jesus refuses to remain on the legal plane. He exposes the origin of each culpable act and thereby accentuates the universal nature of its condemnation,

---

[24] "Ich aber sage euch," in *Der Ruf Jesu und die Antwort* (ed. E. Lohse; Göttingen: Vandenhoeck & Ruprecht, 1970), 189–205; taken up again in his collection *Die Vielfalt des Neuen Testaments* (Göttingen: Vandenhoeck & Ruprecht, 1982).

[25] Literally "have listened," the action upon which the "tradition" rests.

[26] Cf. Str-B 1:253–54.

[27] Merklein, *Jesu Botschaft,* 106–10.

even as he retains the original language of the prohibition. Above all he situates the act under consideration in relation to one's "brother."

Murder and anger (Matt 5:21–26)

[21]You have heard that it was said to those of ancient times, *"You shall not murder";* and "whoever murders shall be liable to judgment."

[22]But I say to you that

if you are angry with a brother, you will be liable to judgment; and if you insult a brother, you will be liable to the council; and if you say, "You fool," you will be liable to the hell of fire. (Matt 5:21–22, NRSV, marg., italics added)

These two verses express Jesus' thinking with regard to the prohibition of murder and the sanctions imposed for homicide in the Jewish tradition. The prohibition is found in the Torah,[28] and the sanction cited here is a loose summary of the different punishments provided for in the law.[29] To this traditional prohibition of murder Jesus adds, with authority, a ban on anger.

In doing this, he sides with the prescriptions of late Judaism that added a ban against vindictive anger to the one on murder.[30] These determined what sanctions to apply on a sliding scale: "The one who calls his neighbor a slave must be banished, and the one who calls him a bastard will receive 40 lashes; but if anyone calls his neighbor an infidel, he may seek his life."[31] Nothing of this kind comes from the mouth of Jesus,

---

[28]Exod 20:13; Deut 5:17.

[29]Exod 21:12; Lev 24:17; Num 35:16–18; Deut 17:8–13. Cf. Str-B 1:254–57.

[30]As in Qumran, for example: 1QS 7:4, 8.

[31]Str-B 1:280.

but his teaching nevertheless presents the paradox of a punishment that is completely out of proportion to the crime. (Was this an ironic comment on the sliding scale we have just illustrated?)

Jesus joins the Torah in identifying anger as the source of murder, but he does so for a different reason. Anger involves a "brother," meaning not just a fellow member of the Christian community, but any person in the whole human community, in whom we can find a "brother" to be loved.[32] Anger is therefore being targeted not as the principal source of homicide, but because it "bears the seeds of the death of brotherly love. It breaks the solidarity with one's neighbor."[33] We should observe that this is not a matter only of the ultimate act, of homicide, but of insults in ordinary life. That being the case, we should recognize that the fifth commandment does not have in view only exceptional situations; it concerns the disciple in day-to-day living.

The words that Jesus adds by way of commentary on the position he is taking confirm this interpretation: two cases taken from daily life are interpreted similarly. The first has to do with not presenting an offering without first being reconciled;[34] the second has to do with an ordinary dispute, and these verses (Matt 5:25–26) seem so artificially placed that they appear to have been taken from Luke:

> [58]Thus, when you go with your accuser before a magistrate, on the way make an effort to settle the case, or you may be dragged before the judge, and the judge hand you over to the officer, and the officer throw you in prison. [59]I tell you, you will never get out until you have paid the very last penny. (Luke 12:58–59)

---

[32]Matt 28:10. Cf. *VTB*, 491–95.
[33]Marguerat, *Le Jugement*, 157, 160.
[34]Matt 5:23–24 (see pp. 51–52).

This saying exhorts the disciple to change his mind before it is too late; Matthew applies it with a catechetical goal in view. He is concerned with maintaining the unity of the Christian community. It applies to cases where I am the one who has done wrong as well as to cases where I have been the victim. It is therefore clear that the focus of my reflections in such cases should not be me, but the other person.

In conclusion, we may recognize that here Jesus breaks with a principle of action that was almost a written law: it is now concern for the other that determines my behavior.

Adultery and lust (Matt 5:27–28)

27You have heard that it was said *"You shall not commit adultery."*

28But I say to you that everyone who *looks at a woman with lust* has already committed adultery with her in his heart. (Matt 5:27–28, italics added)

In Jesus' day, women were considered dangerous beings. It was not appropriate, for example, for a man to speak with a woman alone (John 4:27). At Qumran, it was necessary to abstain from sexual relations. In Islam it is required even today that a man not look at a grown woman. A concern for ritual purity was to preserve men and women from any excess.

The ban on adultery[35] in the Jewish tradition was enforced through very specific legal measures, such as, for example, the requirement that there be witnesses. If Jesus spoke only to the man about looking with lust, this was not to restrict the commandment of the law to him alone, but rather because the man was considered the owner of his wife, as he was the owner of his donkey or his ox.[36]

---

[35]Exod 20:14 = Deut 5:18.
[36]Exod 22:15–16.

The law is not concerned here with lasciviousness, but rather with the social disorder that results when one man desires another's wife. This threatens all propriety, as we see from the case of David, who sent the husband of the woman he desired, Bathsheba, to be killed on the field of battle.[37]

But while the Torah remains on the legal plane, Jesus moves from the outward act to the inner intention, to where the decision originates. This is not only because looking with lust can lead to adultery (this would be classic moralism: one should never put oneself in a situation that could lead easily to sin), but because it is trying to take over the property of another. We today no longer regard women as "objects"; we recognize that they have rights of their own. But Jesus is not really advocating for the "status of women" here, to speak in contemporary terms.

Jesus' saying is paradoxical. It has something other than legal regulation in mind. While its form is legal, its content concerns a "look" that cannot be judged by the law. The principle of action invoked here is not one's relation to the law, but rather one's interior disposition ("in his heart"), which, in itself, escapes from all judgment except God's.

Vows (Matt 5:33–37)

[33]Again, you have heard that it was said to those of ancient times,
"You shall not swear falsely,
but carry out the vows
you have made to the Lord."

[34–36]But I say to you,

Do not swear at all,

either by heaven . . .
or by the earth . . .
or by Jerusalem . . .
and do not swear by your head . . .

---

[37]2 Sam 12.

> [37]Let your word be "Yes, Yes" or "No, No"; anything more than this comes from the evil one. (Matt 5:33–37, italics added)
>
> [Let your "yes" be yes and your "no" be no. (James 5:12)]

Vows are very important in the Bible,[38] not as a means of asking God to testify to what is affirmed, but rather as a means of calling on God to act upon the person speaking. God himself will act to authenticate what has been said. This is the primary meaning of the expression "take the name of God":[39] to ask God to intervene in one's words. This is where the fear of making vows comes from.[40] It also accounts for the various substitutes that are used for the name of God: "By golly" = "by God"; "Oh my gosh" = "Oh my God"; and so forth.[41] A vow is a delicate thing, because by invoking God we incite him to action: is God not truly in the word that is spoken? Thus Jesus proposes a radical measure: no vows at all! In Judaism this measure had already been proposed,[42] but out of fear of perjury.

For Jesus, according to the saying in James 5:12, the thing to do was simply to maintain truthfulness in language, that is, authentic communication, because God will then be in all of our words, the Evil One being in any other kind of speech.

---

[38]Exod 22:10; Judg 8:19; 1 Sam 20:3.

[39]Exod 20:7.

[40]Sir 23:9–10.

[41]The author uses examples from the French language: "Parbleu" = "par Dieu," meaning "by God"; "Jarnieblue" = "Je renie Dieu," "I renounce God"; "Jarnicoton" = "Je renie le Père Coton," "I renounce Father Cotton," a reference to the portrayal of God as white-haired.

[42]Sir 23:9–11, Eccl 5:2.

There was already a saying in the ancient Near East: If subject
and attribute are identical, the language is truthful; if subject
and attribute are contrary, the language is lying.

The disciple of Jesus must speak in absolute truthfulness
and not have to make use of God's name. This will instill mutual confidence among believers. God, after all, should be present in all of our words.

Conclusion

Experiencing God and welcoming God's law

According to Matthew, Jesus contrasted his reading of the
law with that of the scribes. He broke with the chain of interpretations, found in the halakah, that was considered normative. For him, the law was inseparable from the One who had
given it; otherwise his radical standards would be unbearable.
We cannot do without the body of the law, but that body needs
to be continually transformed.

On the one hand, this is a call to perfection: the person
who has taken as the norm of his action God's unconditional
love for his creatures will be devoted unreservedly to the will of
God. Such a person will not give in to anger or to looking with
lust, and will not call on God to make one's sayings more
credible.

As D. Marguerat has so aptly put it, Judaism had "minia-
turized" obedience,[43] but Jesus appealed to the will of God,
sometimes by invoking God's original intentions as Creator[44]
and sometimes by announcing that he would come as Judge at
the end of time.[45] Knowing the beginning and the end allows
us to situate the Law within an overall framework.

---

[43] Matt 15:5–6; 22:24–28; 23:16–18, 23–25.
[44] Matt 5:45; 15:3–6; 19:4, 8.
[45] Matt 5:22, 25–26, 29–30.

In one sense, the teaching of Jesus recenters the law on its primary demand, the commandment to love.[46] Sabbath observance,[47] ceremonial laws, letters of divorce, fasting, the temple tax, vows, the tithe:[48] all of these are valid so long as they do not go against love. Everything culminates with the love of one's enemies.[49]

This is all true, but we must also take into account those sayings in which Jesus requires something specific besides love.[50] Everything really depends not on the law, but on me, on my response to the inbreaking reign of God. The best commentator on the law, Matthew, describes the behavior of Jesus well. He kept the law, but he situated it in relation to the reign of God, which was not just something that was coming, but something that was even then asserting itself. By taking the same position relative to the law as Jesus did, I too can express myself freely and faithfully.

Implications for society

Jesus gave his prescriptions a legal cast that can be misinterpreted. They were not intended to provide a social blueprint, even though some, such as Tolstoy, have attempted to use them that way. Certainly they have important consequences for the social order, but Jesus was not speaking on the level of penal law when, for example, he invited us to "turn the other cheek." The state must defend society against wrongdoers; laws protect it from human excesses. But even if laws are therefore not a detriment, are they sufficient to ensure our happiness?

---

[46] Matt 22:37–40.
[47] Matt 12:1–8, 24:20.
[48] Matt 5:31–32; 6:16–18; 17:24–27; 23:16–22, 23.
[49] Matt 5:43–48.
[50] Matt 19:18–19; 22:37–40; 23:23.

The law according to Jesus

In his declarations about the Torah, Jesus proposed a new way of understanding the law. By making qualitative demands, he addressed us as whole beings: "The eye is the lamp of the body. So, if your eye is healthy, your whole body will be full of light."[51] No hypocrisy is tolerated; it's what's inside that counts.[52] There must therefore be no compromise: "No one can serve two masters."[53] Every stumbling block must be rooted out.[54] We must leave everything to follow Jesus when we have found the treasure or the pearl.[55]

Nothing is qualified anymore: Truthfulness must be absolute; others must be respected without reserve; the Sabbath is made for people; the need for reconciliation takes priority over worship.[56] The commandment to love is the standard by which the law is to be measured.

If love has become the supreme rule, this is because the will of God is no longer identified with the letter of the law and its interpretations. As in Judaism, it is in this or that specific situation that the practice of a given commandment is to be realized. The difference is, in the eyes of Jesus, the "protective hedge" of the Torah is reversed.

Each person is directly confronted by God, his neighbor, and himself. It is through other people that I encounter what God demands of me. What matters is no longer, in Newman's phrase, God and myself, nor is it a matter of "saving my soul," but of living in relationship with my neighbor. This is why forgiveness is so important, as is seeing Christ in

---

51 Matt 6:22.
52 Matt 7:15.
53 Matt 6:24.
54 Mark 9:43–48.
55 Luke 14:26.
56 Matt 5:23–24; Mark 11:25.

the "least of these," not to mention the love that reconciles even enemies.

Where can all of this come from, other than an experience of God-who-is-reigning?

ACCORDING TO THE GOSPEL OF JOHN

The Johannine literature belongs to a profoundly different milieu from the one that the Synoptic tradition assumes. It was written near the end of the first century, at a time when Judaism was regrouping after the destruction of the temple in Jerusalem. It was being renewed thanks to a certain class of Pharisees who gave particular importance to the law of Moses. Christians were then classified among the *minim,* those who were excluded from Jewish worship.

In St. Paul's time, by contrast, there was open competition with the synagogue. The law of Moses presented a temptation to return to the maternal womb and forget the radically new thing that Jesus represented. And so it was said that the law had found its "fulfillment" or had reached its "goal" (Greek *telos*), which could have opened the way to a rejection of the first, foundational covenant.

The Synoptic tradition kept the memory of Jesus of Nazareth alive, striving to show that Jesus protested, with reason, against the abuses of the halakah and revealed the true meaning of the law.

After much reflection and meditation, John presented Jesus as the one in whom God revealed himself as the Father of all humanity. In the process he showed that the law had genuine value, although this value was relative at the same time. It was a preliminary gift of God, whose role needed to be recognized and appreciated. One of its contributions was, in fact, to give birth to a new vocabulary by which the newness of Jesus could be expressed in relation to the law.

Jesus and the Sabbath

Like the Synoptic writers, John describes how Jesus performed miracles on the Sabbath: he healed the lame man at the pool of Bethsaida[57] and the man who was born blind at Jerusalem.[58] On these occasions all the writers bring out the deeper meaning of the Sabbath-rest legislation. But for John, the goal was not simply to proclaim Jesus "Lord of the sabbath."[59] Rather, he declared the deeper meaning of the ban on work:

> My Father is always working, and I also am working.
>   (John 5:17, NRSV, var.)

To justify his actions on the Sabbath,[60] Jesus does not, as in the Synoptics, take the point of view of the law, which is that of his accusers—namely, that the Sabbath rest can legitimately be transgressed out of a deeper faithfulness to the divine intention, for example, when helping a neighbor must take precedence over the ritual prescription. His perspective here in John is completely different. Rather than situating the Sabbath rest in relation to other commandments, Jesus adopts the point of view of God, who is "working until now," in an eschatological present that is literally equivalent to "always."

Jesus raises the sights of his hearers very high: the requirement that people cease from all labor on the seventh day symbolically leaves the whole field to that which God *alone* can accomplish. The healing of the sick, a life-giving work, was one manifestation of God's own action.

By declaring "and I also am working," Jesus places himself unabashedly side by side with God. He does not say, as in

---

[57] John 5:1–47.
[58] John 9:1–38.
[59] Mark 2:28.
[60] Here I am drawing on my *Lecture de l'évangile selon Jean,* 2:35.

the Synoptics, that the Son of Man is Lord of the Sabbath. Rather, on the basis of the unequaled relationship that unites him with his Father, he attributes to himself here an action that has the same permanence and the same content as the divine action. The discourse that follows[61] does not extend this same access to the meaning of the Sabbath to all people; it is rather content to expound the mystery of Jesus' unity with the Father. It is only after chapter 6, which delves more deeply into the mystery of Jesus himself, that the meaning of the Sabbath is taken up again.

Jesus has gone up to the temple in the middle of the Feast of Tabernacles. The Jews are astonished when they hear him teaching and ask themselves if he can be the Christ. Jesus first explains how he is able to speak as he does,[62] and then justifies his healing of the lame man at the pool of Bethsaida by accusing the Jews of not "keeping the law." This is not because they do not observe its precepts, but because they do not have a living relationship with it: they are even seeking to kill him, in the name of the Sabbath!

> [19]"Did not Moses give you the law? Yet none of you keeps the law. Why are you looking for an opportunity to kill me?" [20]The crowd answered, "You have a demon! Who is trying to kill you?" [21]Jesus answered them, "I performed one work, and all of you are astonished. [22]Moses gave you circumcision (it is, of course, not from Moses, but from the patriarchs), and you circumcise a man on the sabbath. [23]If a man receives circumcision on the sabbath in order that the law of Moses may not be broken, are you angry with me because I healed a man's whole body on the sabbath? [24]Do not judge by appearances, but judge with right judgment." (John 7:19–24)

---

[61] John 5:19–47.
[62] John 7:15–18.

In defending himself, Jesus does not reason here as in the Synoptic tradition, by appealing to urgency as a motive, as, for example, in the case of an ox that has fallen into a well.[63] He appeals instead to the practice of circumcising on the Sabbath. In effect, circumcising on the Sabbath is not a legitimate infraction of the law, because it fulfills its fundamental intention. By healing the lame man, Jesus was granting life in its fullness, which is the proper object of the law.

The Fourth Gospel thus presents the law as a gift from God whose purpose is to give life. And this is what Jesus says about it in his discourses.

The Law (Given by Moses) and the Truth

After having shown that all of humanity is illuminated by the Logos and that the Logos entered into the history of a predetermined people, the prologue contrasts the incarnate Logos with the law of Israel in a significant parallelism:

> The law was given through Moses; grace and truth came through Jesus Christ. (John 1:17, NRSV, var.)

To the law corresponds not grace, but truth. The progression is not from law to grace (as the Greek Fathers thought), but from law to truth. This truth surpasses the law, which was only an incomplete manifestation of it; it reveals fully what the God of the covenant had wanted to communicate to Israel ever since her election.

The law is therefore a grace that spreads throughout the whole world. The truth is not simply a gift, it "is," it "was"—these things are said using the same verb as for the incarnation: "The Word became flesh."[64] The history of God's dealings

---

[63] Luke 14:5.

[64] John 1:14. [The verb is *egeneto*.—Trans.]

with humanity culminates with the advent here below of the truth, which is none other than the person of Jesus Christ. But in this history, Moses and the law nevertheless occupy a privileged position.

The Law, a Gift of God to Bring Life

The Greek term *nomos,* which John uses freely, does not refer only to a body of legislation. It can indicate the Pentateuch, a legal principle or the teaching of Moses, with the whole of the Scriptures always in view.[65] The law is the manna on which the Israelite must feed in order to live. This is what the reaction of the Jews shows, when they meet Jesus after the miracle of the multiplication of the loaves:

> [26]"You are looking for me, not because you saw signs, but because you ate your fill of the loaves. [27]Do not work for the food that perishes, but for the food that endures for eternal life, which the Son of Man will give you. For it is on him that God the Father has set his seal." [28]Then they said to him, "What must we do to perform the works of God?" [29]Jesus answered them, "This is the work of God, that you believe in him whom he has sent." (John 6:26–29)

The Jews move spontaneously from the gift of the loaves to the work of performing the law. They understand that the coriander seeds scattered over the surface of the desert represent the law, in which Israel is to find its nourishment each day. They believe that Jesus is able to give them the bread (the true law) on which they want to live:

> [32]Then Jesus said to them, "Very truly, I tell you, it was not Moses who gave you the bread from heaven, but it is my Father who gives you the true bread from heaven. [33]For the bread of

---

[65]John 1:17, 45; 7:19, 23, 49, 51; 8:17; 10:34; 12:34; 15:25; 19:7.

God is he who comes down from heaven and gives life to the world." [34]They said to him, "Sir, give us this bread always." (John 6:32–34, NRSV, marg.)

The law is thus seen as the way that leads to life. It requires that its commandments be put into practice, and it requires particularly an openness to whatever situation might present itself. Jesus deplored the absence of this attitude among his contemporaries:

Did not Moses give you the law? Yet none of you keeps the law. Why are you looking for an opportunity to kill me? (John 7:19)

While Jesus tried to renew the true sense of the law by bringing life to the paralyzed man, the Jews, for their part, were not practicing the law. This was not because they were disobeying one commandment or another, but because they were opposing life and seeking death. The conflict between them did not have to do with practicing the commandments, but rather with the meaning of the law: life.

The Law Is Fulfilled in the Truth

Some would declare, with Paul, that Jesus put an end to the law, but Jesus himself avoided saying that he would replace the law. This would have been to declare that the law lost its meaning the moment the One came in whom all things find their origin and their destiny. The law had more than a transitory role; it has an enduring function, even in the midst of its own fulfillment. What is this function? The answer can be found in the transpositions that John makes.

The term *nomos* seems to be reserved in the rest of the gospel for the law of Moses as a whole, while the term *entolē* now appears and is used to designate the various commandments that make up the law. Jesus uses the term himself:

> ¹⁷For this reason the Father loves me, because I lay down my life in order to take it up again. ¹⁸No one takes it from me, but I lay it down of my own accord. I have power to lay it down, and I have power to take it up again. I have received this command from my Father. (John 10:16–17)

The "it is necessary" that characterizes the places in the Synoptics where it is said that the Son of Man must die and rise again is transposed into the final declaration here, "I have received this command from my Father." But there is an initial affirmation that parallels this declaration: "the Father loves me." Thus two propositions are affirmed and distinguished from one another: the commandment received from the Father, and the perfect liberty of the Son. From the two persons gushes forth a perfect unity of action. But the notion of the commandment is indispensable to express duality in the midst of this perfect unity.

The New Commandment

The same dual expression characterizes the relationship that unites the believer to Jesus. It was by means of a commandment that Jesus asked his disciples to love one another:

> I give you a new commandment, that you love one another. Just as I have loved you, you also should love one another. (John 13:34)

The love of the Son for his disciples generates their impulse of love: it is his love that passes through them when they love their brothers and are loved by them. To ensure that this love among the disciples is the fruit of Jesus' word, the term "commandment" is used to underscore that the disciple, by himself, is not the only doer of his own act; it is rather the product of a "synergy."[66]

---

[66]I return here to my *Lecture de l'évangile selon Jean,* 3:80–85.

The same observations can be made about the instructions given to the individual disciple:

> If you love me, you will keep my commandments. (14:15)

> They who have my commandments and keep them are those who love me. (14:21)

> Those who love me will keep my word. (14:23)

> Whoever does not love me does not keep my words. (14:24)

The sequence in vv. 14–24 proves to be structured not by the verb "love" alone, but by the pair "love/keep," whose respective objects are Jesus and his commandments (or his word). This pair comes to John from the Deuteronomic tradition: loving God (that is, being attached to his will) and keeping his commandments are one and the same thing for Israel, which was called into the covenant. By giving "commandments" the same significance as "words," John shows that he is faithful to the Deuteronomic tradition, in which the law is above all a divine revelation that leads to life. The Decalogue is sometimes referred to as the "Ten Words"; what Jesus calls "my" commandments are in fact those of the Father.

In the final analysis, all of this presupposes a certain reality: not of God as an individual, but of the relationship between the Father and the Son, which is the basis of the relationship between the disciple and Jesus. Such is the connection between *two* and *one*. God-who-reigns is God the Father, whom we learned from John (see ch. 1) is both identical with and different from the Son.

Chapter 3

Humanity in Relation to God-Who-Is-Coming

When he announced that the reign of God had drawn near, Jesus showed that he was in the presence of God in a special way; indeed, he himself proved to *be* the presence of God. But this announcement was also a challenge that he posed to his contemporaries, which he still poses to everyone today.

A response of a ritual nature can be offered by the community, in the form of temples where we hope to see God dwelling among us. It can also be of a personal nature, through prayer, by which we hope to enter into dialogue with God. But such is not the object of our present inquiry. We seek only to examine *how every person should act morally* according to the gospel.

If Jesus' criterion of action was no longer the law as such, but simply the experience of God-at-work, why should it not still be the same for those who believe in him? If we refuse to welcome God, who is still coming today, we produce actions that do not express what we are destined for. However, if we

welcome God-who-is-coming today, we can act fully. We will
see that a true *synergy* can exist between God and ourselves.

ACCORDING TO THE SYNOPTIC TRADITION

Humanity Has Become Wicked

Human persons are beings who have always been dependent on God for our every breath. But now God comes to
us in a new way. By announcing that "the reign of God has
drawn near," Jesus invites us to welcome him. However, contrary to everything we might expect, the gospel writers seem to
take satisfaction in relating how Jesus was rejected. This fact
may discourage the reader, and so it is appropriate to situate it
in relation to the end of the story, that is, the triumph of life
over death. For it is death we must confront in order to
appreciate life.

Humanity does not welcome the message

Even if historians describe the first part of Jesus' ministry
as the "Galilean spring," the gospel writers do not present it as
such. After Jesus' earliest encounters with the Jewish people,
"the Pharisees went out and immediately conspired with the
Herodians against him, how to destroy him."[1] The gospel writers may be simplifying the situation, as it is likely that these
leaders showed such animosity toward Jesus only later. Nevertheless, their accounts reflect a reality.

If, for their part, the religious and political leaders were
suspicious of the actions and preaching of this newcomer, neither were the people as a whole, for their part, "converted to his
word," any more than to that of John the Baptist.[2] The cities of

---

[1] Mark 3:6.
[2] Matt 11:16–19 = Luke 7:29–35.

Galilee were not converted when they saw Jesus' miracles,[3] nor was Jerusalem, even though Jesus wanted to gather her to himself "as a hen gathers her brood under her wings."[4] Jesus therefore had to admit that he had failed to make himself understood.

The same admission of defeat had to be made in the case of the disciples, whose "lack of faith" Jesus criticized to the point where he included them in the "faithless generation" that was so "hard to put up with."[5] They were always wanting to do things like call fire down from heaven on an inhospitable Samaritan village.[6] Even when the risen Christ "spoke to them about the reign of God," their surprising question to him was, "Lord, is this the time when you will restore the [political] kingdom to Israel?" Jesus does not reprimand them; it is enough for him to challenge their desire to "know the times or periods that the Father has set by his own authority"[7] and to announce the coming of the Holy Spirit. What is this, if not another admission of defeat? While he was living on earth, when the Spirit had not yet been given, Jesus was not able to make the spiritual message of the reign of God understood. Nor was he able to communicate that his life was not simply terrestrial, but that it expressed the very life of God.

Jesus himself was not deceived by the success his preaching enjoyed at the beginning. He expressed this through the parable of the Sower:[8]

---

[3] Matt 11:20–24 = Luke 10:12–15.
[4] Matt 23:37 = Luke 13:34.
[5] Mark 9:19 and pars.
[6] Luke 9:54–55.
[7] Acts 1:6–7.
[8] See my interpretation of Matthew's version in *Études d'évangile*, 255–301.

³Listen! A sower went out to sow. ⁴And as he sowed, some seeds fell on the path, and the birds came and ate them up. ⁵Other seeds fell on rocky ground, where they did not have much soil, and they sprang up quickly, since they had no depth of soil. ⁶But when the sun rose, they were scorched; and since they had no root, they withered away. ⁷Other seeds fell among thorns, and the thorns grew up and choked them. ⁸Other seeds fell on good soil and brought forth grain, some a hundredfold, some sixty, some thirty. ⁹Let anyone with ears listen! (Matt 13:3–9)

Jesus relates here the story of his coming into the world, the story of the reception the divine Seed experienced among the people of God. He came announcing the arrival of the reign of God. Some shut out this proclamation: the "wise" and the powerful, the Pharisees who attributed to Beelzebul the exorcisms by which Jesus cast out demons. Others listened but did not produce the fruits of conversion; the inhabitants of Capernaum and Chorazin, or those whom Jesus described as singing or crying at the wrong times, were among this group. But there were others, if only a handful, who listened with their whole hearts and followed Jesus.⁹ The eschatological moment had arrived: God scattered the seed, the encounter took place. It was up to the people to be the good soil and to open themselves to the seed so that it might bear fruit among them.

If the call was not answered, neither was the proclamation itself properly understood. In the phrase "the *basilea* of God is at hand," the original Aramaic term *malkutah* is ambiguous. It can mean both the *reign* that God exercises in history—now the generally accepted sense of what Jesus meant—and the *kingdom* that will be established at the end of time. When Jesus proclaimed that the reign of God had drawn

---

⁹Matt 12:24; 11:20–24; 11:16–17; 5:1–7:28.

near, he was understood as announcing that the kingdom would soon be established, even though it was only present in Jesus himself.

Have not those Christians who have identified the kingdom to come with the church of the present fallen into the same illusion as those Jews who imagined that Jesus wanted to establish the kingdom of God on earth? John makes clear that the Galileans who were so enthusiastic about the multiplication of the loaves had a political motive: "This is indeed the prophet who is to come into the world." He also records Jesus' reaction: "When Jesus realized that they were about to come and take him by force to make him king, he withdrew again to the mountain by himself."[10] No, Jesus did not want to establish the kingdom of God on earth through political means.

Jesus refused to be acclaimed king in the political sense of the word, most clearly at the time of his triumphal entry into Jerusalem.[11] Nevertheless, according to the inscription above his cross, it was as such a king that he was crucified: "Jesus of Nazareth, King of the Jews."[12] This inscription served two purposes. Through it, Pilate mocked the people of Israel, presenting a miserable individual to them as their king. But at the same time, it invites believers to acknowledge in this king their crucified Messiah.[13] That the concept of "king" could have such a double meaning shows the paradoxical character of Jesus' message.

---

[10]John 6:14–15. John's account is of historical value, as it harmonizes with the strange fact mentioned in the synoptic tradition: "Immediately he made his disciples get into the boat" (Mark 6:45 and pars.).

[11]Matt 21:5 = Luke 19:38.

[12]Matt 27:37 = Mark 15:26 = Luke 23:38 = John 19:19. See my book *Lecture de l'évangile selon Jean* (Paris: Seuil, 1996), 4:118.

[13]1 Cor 1:23; Gal 3:1. This reading is influenced by the Fourth Gospel, but it is rooted in synoptic soil.

This paradox was not new. It was the distinguishing characteristic of the religion of Israel. When he made his covenant
with Israel, God promised earthly happiness with the coming
of the Messiah: life, peace, justice. But he specified some conditions at the same time.

Deuteronomy emphasized the radical demands of God:
there were to be no halfway measures when it came to obeying
the commandments! It was a choice between life and death. In
concrete terms, believers maintains their existence by being
nourished by this world's goods, but they must recognize that
this "having" is only given to them for the sake of their "being,"
a being that comes from God alone.

In the prophetic tradition God is portrayed as uncompro-
mising: he will not tolerate any "rival." "I am God, and there is
no other" is the prophetic refrain. Israel, however, never ceased
to depend on creatures that were, in the eyes of God, nothing
more than "idols." In the eyes of Jesus' contemporaries, the
covenant God made with them had become a *reciprocal contract,* according to which the believer's conduct would be re-
warded as if by an actual salary. But what kind of salary? One
determined by human standards or by God's?

In one of Jesus' parables, the master of a vineyard hires
workers at different times of day, agreeing with each one for a
whole day's pay. When the time comes to pay the workers, he
gives notice that the salary will not be based on the amount of
work done, but will correspond to the original agreement. As a
result, those who did the most work murmur against the
landowner.

> [12]"These last worked only one hour, and you have made them
> equal to us who have borne the burden of the day and the
> scorching heat." [13]But he replied to one of them, "Friend, I am
> doing you no wrong; did you not agree with me for the usual
> daily wage? [14]Take what belongs to you and go; I choose to

give to this last the same as I give to you. [15]Am I not allowed to do what I choose with what belongs to me? Or are you envious because I am generous?" (Matt 20:12–15)

No one can "deserve" eternal life as recompense for some performance. God's justice cannot be measured according to the distributive justice of humanity. Rather, everything is determined by God's goodness.

Each person is but a "servant"

Jesus reduces the condition of humanity even further: we are nothing more than servants. This comparison is radically disturbing:

> [7]Who among you would say to your slave who has just come in from plowing or tending sheep in the field, "Come here at once and take your place at the table"? [8]Would you not rather say to him, "Prepare supper for me, put on your apron and serve me while I eat and drink; later you may eat and drink"? [9]Do you thank the slave for doing what was commanded? [10]So you also, when you have done all that you were ordered to do, say, "We are worthless slaves; we have done only what we ought to have done!" (Luke 17:7–10)

Today we are so egalitarian in our thinking that we are understandably indignant when we hear this. We fail to appreciate that the relationship that unites us to God is not of the same nature as relationships between people. We really have no rights before God; we cannot lay claim to any consideration whatever when it comes to our condition before God. We cannot unionize to protect our "rights" against God! We are, quite properly, servants; that is what the original formula means: "We are worthless slaves" (*achreioi*), an expression that may be translated "we are *only* slaves." Even though we are invited to cooperate in our salvation, we cannot produce it.

Each person is a sinner

In Jesus' perspective, God has drawn near to every person. But each individual must recognize that he or she is a pardoned "sinner": for Jesus says,

> I have come to call not the righteous but sinners. (Matt 9:13 = Mark 2:17)

Such is the unconditional pardon that will henceforth be granted to those who welcome the announcement of the reign of God. Jesus proclaims this forcefully in opposition to those who, in keeping with the Jewish principle of retribution,[14] believed in a cause-and-effect relationship between misfortune and one's actions. In their view, every misfortune represented divine punishment for some wrongdoing. Jesus' own attitude is best understood by his response to the news of a catastrophe:

> [1]At that very time there were some present who told him about the Galileans whose blood Pilate had mingled with their sacrifices. [2]He asked them, "Do you think that because these Galileans suffered in this way they were worse sinners than all other Galileans? [3]No, I tell you; but unless you repent, you will all perish [apoleisthe] as they did. [4]Or those eighteen who were killed [apekteinen] when the tower of Siloam fell on them—do you think that they were worse offenders than all the others living in Jerusalem? [5]No, I tell you; but unless you repent, you will all perish just as they did." (Luke 13:1–5)

The anecdote, which is considered historical,[15] reveals very clearly what Jesus' attitude was toward the connection

---

[14] This way of thinking was common in the time of Jesus; we read in John 9:2, "His disciples asked him, 'Rabbi, who sinned, this man or his parents, that he was born blind?'" Cf. Str-B 2:193–94.

[15] The case for this is made in note 22 of my book *Face à la mort,* 33. Pilate's brutality was notorious (Flavius Josephus, *Jewish Antiquities* 18, 4, 1).

that is often drawn between guilt and violent death. "Job's friends" were trying to argue for just such a connection.[16] Before anything else, Jesus wants to make his interlocutors admit their belief that Pilate's victims, or those of the collapse of the tower of Siloam, had to have been "worse sinners" or "worse offenders" than the survivors. This, they felt, was the only way to make sense of their deaths. But it is impossible to establish any correlation between a *given* misfortune and a *given* sin.[17]

After making this essential clarification, Jesus invites his listeners to consider the implications for their own lives. They should not be speculating about what each of the victims might have done, nor congratulating themselves by saying, "Well, at least I was spared." They should rather be actively questioning themselves. Rather than lingering over the tragedy, they should be giving their attention to the reign of God that Jesus is announcing by his words and deeds. They should be trying to discern the *kairos,* the "time designated"[18] by the reign of God that has come. This is what Jesus tells them in a saying that is cited just before the passage we have been considering:

> You hypocrites! You know how to interpret the appearance of earth and sky, but why do you not know how to interpret the present time? (Luke 12:56)

If the time of the reign of God has truly arrived, then humanity must "be converted," meaning that we must not just listen to the message of Jesus, but above all recognize that we are "sinners." This is the first condition we must meet in order not to "perish," a term that is used here in a sense that ordinarily has

---

[16] For example, in Job 8.

[17] I developed this theme in *Face à la mort,* 3d ed. (1973), 34–35.

[18] By contrast with *chronos,* which indicates "successive time," *kairos* indicates a "designated time." Cf. *DNT,* 522–23.

in view not mortal death (designated by the verb *apokteinō*) but being sent without hope of return into the abode of the dead (*apollumi*).

Jesus refused to tie together sin and tragic death. On the other hand, he revealed that an unseen link unites sin with spiritual perdition. And just as Jesus called everyone to conversion, he made it clear that every person is a sinner, thus anticipating the reflections of St. Paul and St. John on the "sin of the world," that is, the collective dimension of every individual sin. The universe is a "broken world." In order to welcome the reign of God, we must recognize that we are sinners, not for the sake of wallowing in a sense of guilt, but to be open to God, who is always disposed to grant his pardon.

Humanity is "evil"

Jesus was deeply convinced that we must consider ourselves servants, and even sinners. He speaks of this in various ways, but he does so continually. To the rich man who gave Jesus the title "Good Master," Jesus retorted brusquely:

> Why do you call me good? No one is good but God alone. (Mark 10:18)

This means that, except for God, everyone is "evil":

> If you then, who are evil, know how to give good gifts to your children . . . (Matt 7:11 = Luke 11:13)

> An evil and adulterous generation asks for a sign. (Matt 12:39 = Luke 11:29)

The use of the term "evil" must be properly understood. For a Jew, to call someone evil was not to devalue that person as a creature of God, but given that a covenant has been made with God, a person becomes "evil" as soon as he or she ceases to observe the law. This was the Pharisee's accusation against the publican: was not observance of the law the essential condition for salvation? For Jesus, in keeping with the long biblical tradition, all people are "evil," not by nature, but because they are sinners, unfaithful to the law.

> Every inclination of the thoughts of their hearts was only evil continually. (Gen 6:5)

> Indeed, I was born guilty, a sinner when my mother conceived me. (Ps 51:5)

The idea here is certainly not that sin is transmitted in the sexual act, which was considered to be evil in itself. Nor is there a concept of "original sin" in the current theological sense of that term. Nevertheless, the door is open for the universality of sin, since the covenant with God has been broken by humanity. If, therefore, Jesus is among us, it is not to confirm the "righteous" in their presumption, but to invite "sinners" to welcome God, who, in his person, has come to restore the covenant.

Not that humanity, by our actions, provoked God to intervene. Certainly the goodness of God is ready to shine forth from us, since we are the "image of God." But *from ourselves without God* can spring only bad things. We must "be converted." But what does this mean? It does not mean primarily "doing" something, but rather welcoming the boundless mercy of God, such as was demonstrated by the father of the prodigal son.[19] Thus God is there, waiting for us to recognize and acknowledge genuinely that we are only servants and sinners.

Little Children Are at Home in the Reign of God

This brief inquiry has been sufficient to show clearly that the demands of Jesus are such that it is almost impossible to welcome his message. Is this why the gospel writers

---

[19] Luke 15:20–24.

emphasized that, from the beginning of Jesus' life, his message was never welcomed in its entirety?

The Father has revealed the message to little children

The presentation of the gospel message is not halted by setbacks; Jesus affirmed that even if the seed is in large part lost, it nevertheless bears much fruit. We have already seen this in the parable of the Sower.[20]

Matthew understands a saying of Jesus to proclaim this confidently, since he places it just after a description of the setbacks Jesus experienced in Galilee:

> [25]At that time Jesus said, "I thank you, Father, Lord of heaven and earth, because you have hidden these things from the wise and the intelligent and have revealed them to infants; [26]yes, Father, for such was your gracious will." (Matt 11:25–26 = Luke 10:21)

Jesus, in perfect union with the Father, who disposes all things, thus proclaims that his message has been understood by "infants."[21] These are people who are clearly distinguished from the "wise and intelligent," meaning those who possess an understanding of the law; they are "simple," not because they are humble, but because they are not able to rely on themselves. The term applies well to children, who by their very nature are poor.

Blessed are the poor!

Jesus effectively expressed the same truth in a different way when he said that the "poor" were blessed:

> Blessed are the poor in spirit, for theirs is the kingdom of heaven. (Matt 5:3)

---

[20] See above, pp. 73–74.

[21] Cf. Simon Légasse, *Jésus et l'enfant* (Paris: Gabalda, 1969), 121–85.

This proclamation is often misinterpreted, depending on whether, by appeal to Luke's version alone, the social aspect of poverty as opposed to wealth is exclusively emphasized, or whether, by appeal to Matthew alone, only the interior virtue of simplicity is retained. It is therefore appropriate for us to linger a bit over the terms in this beatitude.

First of all, when he used the term "blessed" (*makarioi*), Jesus was not pronouncing a "blessing"; he was specifying a state.[22] In the same way, he does not "curse" those who are rich; he rather characterizes them as "unfortunate."[23]

The "poor" (*ptōkoi* in Greek) should not be identified as "paupers" (*rach* in Hebrew), nor as "covetous,"[24] nor as "weak" (Hebrew *dal*),[25] nor as the "crushed" whose vigor is so diminished they curl up like sleeping dogs. Rather, they should be identified with the *anawim,* those beings who are bent low and who, unable to obtain justice for themselves, cry out for it to God, their only defender. Each of the gospel writers explains this term "poor" in his own way, by means of the beatitudes that follow. The poor are those who are hungry, who weep, who are persecuted; the truly unfortunate ones, however, are those who are rich and satisfied, who laugh, who are admired by others.

Sociologists insist that there will inevitably be poor people who are oppressed by the rich. But religious thinkers, beginning with Jesus in the prophetic tradition, have judged this

---

[22] Cf. Ps 1:1. Jacques Dupont has treated the entire subject magnificently in three volumes: *Les Béatitudes* (Bruges: Abbaye de Saint-André, 1958–1973).

[23] Luke 6:24–26.

[24] Hebrew *ebyon,* Greek *penēs,* Exod 23:6, 11; Prov 30:7–9.

[25] The "thin cows" of Gen 41:19 or the "poorest of the land" in Jer 40:7.

unacceptable.[26] The land of Israel belongs to God, who is its king.[27] He is therefore the one who maintains justice and delivers the oppressed. This is the source of the declarations in favor of the poor repeated by the prophets of old.[28] But as the situation of the poor did not change, the prophets, speaking as those who had a direct experience of God rather than as representatives of an official religious institution,[29] projected their hopes into the future that God would bring. The monks of Qumran, for their part, identified the poor with those who observed the law.[30] Little by little the "spirit of poverty" thus came to be admired.

Jesus, for his part, belongs to the eschatological tradition of the prophets and is thus full of concern for the poor. However, he considers them poor not because of their virtue, but only because of their state, which is both a sociological and religious one: the poor are those who place their hope completely outside themselves. They are the "clients of God."[31] We could even translate Jesus' saying this way: "Blessed are the clients of God, those who have nothing but God himself," like the poor widow whom Jesus praised.[32]

This is why Jesus himself had for clients the forsaken, the outcasts, the despised, the sick, the possessed, women, and

---

[26] Pss 10:8–10; 12:1–6; 73:4; 94:5–6, 21. Dupont records a good number of Middle Eastern texts that condemn this state of affairs (*Les Béatitudes,* 2:54–80).

[27] Isa 9:6; 11:2–5; Ps 72:3; 10–14. Cf. Dupont, *Les Béatitudes,* 2:86–87.

[28] Exod 22:24–26; cf. Amos 2:6–10; Deut 15:7–11, 12–18; 23:20–25; 24:6, 14–15.

[29] Amos 1:2; 3:8; 7:15.

[30] *1QH [Qumran Hymns]* 5:22. Cf. Dupont, *Les Béatitudes,* 2:72.

[31] Marie-Joseph Lagrange, *Évangile selon saint Luc* (Paris: Gabalda, 1948), 187.

[32] Mark 12:41–44 and pars.

children. He did not issue a prophetic appeal for an apocalyptic political revolution, but he nevertheless announced the overthrow of earthly values: from that moment on, the kingdom of God which was to come was meant for all the poor. There was still one genuine requirement to fulfill, but it was no longer the ability to meet all the demands of the law. Rather, it was to welcome the reign of God, or, more exactly, to welcome God who was coming to save unconditionally.

According to Luke, the poor and the persecuted are declared "very happy," blessed. According to Matthew, the blessed are those who live in spiritual poverty. Each of these blessings is certainly valid, but if taken in isolation, they can sometimes lead to excesses. The text of Luke can be used to disguise a humanistic sociologism[33] that would make the poor the "magi" of history. An appeal to Matthew alone can tend to reduce authentic spiritual poverty to a vague "spirit of poverty" that can coexist quite comfortably with a neglect of the poor.

We should also always bear in mind the religious dimension of Jesus' proclamation. The "poor" he is thinking of are certainly people who are in need, but their need has a religious dimension. These are the heirs of the *anawim,* the poor who cry out to God, their only defender; whose voices are heard, after the return from the exile, with vehemence in the psalms that religious people still sing today: they are the "poor in heart."

Children, models of how to enter the kingdom

Even though Jesus blessed the little children, he did not thereby affirm that the reign of God belonged to them.

---

[33] I have chosen to render literally the author's term *sociologisme,* meaning the theory that sociology can account for all the data that society presents, independently of psychology and other scientific disciplines.—Trans.

Nevertheless, he held them up to his disciples as living models for them to imitate. In what sense?

Most readers of the Gospels continue to follow the traditional interpretation, which the scholarly consensus also reflects:[34] children are obedient and trusting, they provide an example of availability and are to be admired for their simplicity, innocence, and even humility. But the biblical perspective is quite different: children are a sign of divine blessing and must be exposed to the realities of the faith, first by their parents and then by their teachers until they reach the age of religious majority (twelve years old for girls, thirteen years old for boys), which is to be celebrated by a *bat* or *bar mitzvah* in keeping with the law, because they represent the future of the chosen people. While they are never cited for their innocence, they are afflicted like everyone else with the common failing: they are without understanding.[35]

In the eyes of Jesus, children are significant, not because of their innocence, nor because of their humility, and not even as an anticipation of Israel's hoped-for future, but because of their capacity to welcome. Jesus received little children, unlike his disciples, who tried to turn them away:

> [13]People were bringing little children to him in order that he might touch them; and the disciples spoke sternly to them. [14]But when Jesus saw this, he was indignant and said to them, "Let the little children come to me; do not stop them; for it is to such as these that the kingdom of God belongs. [15]Truly I tell you, whoever does not receive the kingdom of God as a little child will never enter it." [16]And he took them up in his arms, laid his hands on them, and blessed them. (Mark 10:13–16)

---

[34] Cf. Légasse, *Jésus et l'enfant,* 269–87.
[35] Wis 12:24.

Jesus took in his arms and blessed those who had no privileges according to the law, no doubt because they were so disposed to welcome others. This disposition makes children a model of the behavior Jesus expects of everyone.

The idea of "welcoming the reign" implies a personal response that connects the one who welcomes with the one who gives. Early Christianity freely used similar formulas.[36] The verb "welcome" describes our roles: not to do something to seize the reign, but to become disposed to receive it as a gift. Welcoming the reign of God is analogous to the relationship between grace and free will. In any good deed, everything is of God, and everything is of humanity. It is not possible to distinguish which parts of the action belong to each of them. However, we can recognize their separate roles: the gift and the grace are God's part; our part is to welcome.[37]

So Jesus invites us to welcome the reign of God, and another saying of his permits us to specify of what this welcome consists. The saying is transmitted by two traditions that are probably mutually independent. According to Mark, we must imitate children who welcome, but according to Matthew, we must also "change and become like them."[38]

Truly I tell you, whoever does not receive the kingdom of God as a little child will never enter it. (Mark 10:15)	[3]Truly I tell you, unless you change and become like children you will never enter the kingdom of heaven. [4]Whoever becomes humble like this child is the greatest in the kingdom of heaven. (Matt 18:3–4)

---

[36]*Dechomai:* Acts 8:14; 11:1; 17:11; 1 Thess 1:6; 2:13.

[37]I agree on this point with Mme. Lot-Borodine. I have treated this subject in "Grâce et libre arbitre chez saint Augustin," *RSR* 33 (1946): 129–63.

[38]John (3:3, 5) carries this need for transformation even further by declaring that we must be "born again."

Matthew, in his version of v. 3, adds the idea that change is a condition of entering the kingdom of God. In v. 4 he gives an explanation: one must "humble oneself" (*tapeinōsei*) to the level of a child. Jesus requires his disciples to make an effort at "turnaround," which here is probably not the equivalent of a "conversion," but simply an invitation to present themselves as children would, without pretension. But does this mean that disciples must renounce their capacity as adults, or simply that they must not put on airs?

For Matthew as for Mark, the disciple of Jesus must act "like a little child" in order to be able to enter the kingdom of heaven. But Matthew makes the requirement for kingdom entrance stricter: it is not enough to think of ourselves as imitating the actions of children; we need to "change and become like little children" (Matt 18:3). The requirement is strict because the child whom we are to emulate has no rights, except that of being loved.

Christian Action

Disciples must act

When believers meet God and recognize his intentions, we welcome the covenant by doing something. We must "enter by the narrow gate,"[39] that is, by avoiding the obstacles we will discuss shortly—the love of money, confidence in our own merits—and by seeking to fulfill the radical demands of the Sermon on the Mount. True disciples will not be content with fine words; we will put them into practice.

> Not everyone who says to me, "Lord, Lord," will enter the kingdom of heaven, but only the one who does the will of my Father in heaven. (Matt 7:21 = Luke 6:46)

---

[39] Matt 7:13 = Luke 13:24.

Everyone then who hears these words of mine and acts on them will be like a wise man who built his house on rock. (Matt 7:24 = Luke 6:47)

Many are the texts in which Jesus delineates the conditions of an authentic welcome. The analogy of the tree and the good fruit describes them well:

> [43]No good tree bears bad fruit, nor again does a bad tree bear good fruit; [44]for each tree is known by its own fruit. Figs are not gathered from thorns, nor are grapes picked from a bramble bush. [45]The good person out of the good treasure of the heart produces good, and the evil person out of evil treasure produces evil; for it is out of the abundance of the heart that the mouth speaks. [46]Why do you call me "Lord, Lord," and do not do what I tell you? (Luke 6:43–46)[40]

Through this appeal to common sense, Jesus underscores the need for the disciple to have welcomed the good news of God-who-reigns today. It follows that the act of the believer must be a divine act. In the life of Jesus himself, the same situation prevailed. Some came to Jesus even though they did not keep the law, while the "practitioners" who did not listen either to John the Baptist or to Jesus were shut out from the kingdom. This is what the parable of the two sons teaches.[41] The comment on it is considered an authentic saying of Jesus:[42]

> Truly I tell you, the tax collectors and the prostitutes are going into the kingdom of God ahead of you [*proagousin*]. (Matt 21:31)

We need to understand these words in the polemical context in which Jesus lived. Those he was speaking to were not merely

---

[40]According to the critics, this sequence of sayings comes from the Q-source (cf. Merklein, 136).

[41]Matt 21:28–31.

[42]Schlosser, *Le règne de Dieu,* 451–76.

"preceded" by the tax collectors and prostitutes; they were "left behind." This is the meaning that the Aramaic term underlying the verb *proagousin* provides.[43] The saying is shocking, but Jesus has in mind that the future beneficiaries of the kingdom will be those who have put his word into practice.

The nature of the action required of the disciple is specified in the parable of the Talents.[44] The talent received from the master must be made to bear fruit. This is what the good servants did. However, it is also necessary not to be afraid to "risk," for example, by "investing the money with bankers." The wicked servant was not, properly speaking, lazy; he was "craven."[45]

Believers must act "morally"

This brings us to the theme of "moral action." According to the theological manuals, action is said to be moral when it is in keeping with the commandments of God. This was also the Jewish conception, but for Jesus, the criterion for moral action goes beyond this. In the preceding chapter, we examined Jesus' relationship to the law, and we concluded that by placing his emphasis on God-who-reigns, Jesus changed everything.

Even though humanity is "good for nothing" when it comes to obtaining salvation, it does not follow that we are excused from acting. The fact that God encounters us should not be understood to mean that God alone is active in regard to us who remain passive. It is God, after all, who makes us moral beings.

---

[43] J. Jeremias, *Les paraboles de Jésus* (French translation; Lyon: Mappus, 1982), 462. English translation: *The Parables of Jesus* (trans. from the German by S. H. Hooke; 2d ed.; New York: Scribner, 1972). Schlosser has taken up and developed this conclusion (*Le regne de Dieu*, 126n2).

[44] Matt 24:14–30.

[45] Matt 25:26, as in the second edition of the *TOB*. The adjective *oknēros* appears only here in the New Testament, and it shapes the overall meaning of the parable: we need to know how to take risks.

There is an authentic human action, because it is *at the same time* the action of God. Such is the paradox of our "action." Catholic teaching likes to promote the role of grace, which transforms human action. I prefer to retain the language of the Orthodox, who for their part speak of *synergy* when it comes to our religious action.

This raises some other questions, for example, that of our motivation for acting. Toward what end do we intend an action? Is it disinterested, or motivated by some future reward? Is it imposed from the outside, or produced from within? Is my action ruled by a fear of punishment, or a desire for reward? It is easy to imagine that Jesus expected his disciples to act with radical freedom when it came to punishments and future rewards. To what extent is this true?

1. Jesus frequently predicted that those who did not welcome the reign of God-who-was-coming would suffer a *judgment of condemnation*. Because the inhabitants of Chorazin and Bethsaida did not recognize, from the miracles that took place in their midst, that Jesus of Nazareth had come on God's behalf to announce the good news of salvation,[46] he told them, "On the day of judgment it will be more tolerable for the land of Sodom than for you."[47]

Nevertheless, Jesus speaks of this judgment in an entirely different manner than John the Baptist did. For John, the judgment would be of Israel in its entirety,[48] and the One who was coming was threatening: the chaff would be burned with unquenchable fire.[49] While Jesus also speaks of what is "to come," this is no longer judgment but salvation. And for him the judgment will be of those who, once having welcomed the reign

---

[46] Luke 10:13–15 and pars.
[47] Matt 11:24.
[48] Matt 3:7, 9.
[49] Matt 3:12.

of God, have not been careful to act in the way Jesus has invited them to. The future is not consumed by God's present;
rather, it makes anyone whom God has encountered keen with
anticipation.

An awareness of judgment should not lead us to live in
fear, but it should awaken in us a sense of how serious it is to
encounter God-who-is-coming. In the words of Angèle de
Foligno, "God doesn't love us just for fun."

2. On the other hand, the idea of a *reward* has a promi-
nent place in Jesus' message. This surprises us less and less the
more we understand what he meant by this.

When it is a matter of humans relating to one another,
interchanges take the form of a contract between two equal
parties, to the point where we can speak freely of them as
"commerce." Retribution is a matter of justice: every action has
an appropriate consequence. But the situation is quite different when it is a matter of people relating to God. In this case
the two partners are not equal.

The terminology is significant in this regard: rather than
being content to use the term "covenant" to describe the relationship God established with his people, the Greek translation known as the Septuagint spoke of a "testament" by which
God made a gift of his person and his goods to his partner.
Even though, under the first covenant, God promised the rewards of health, land, and earthly happiness, these were but a
foretaste of God's gift of his own person. (All of this notwith-
standing, however, we still hear the language of retribution.)

Even though the divine reward does not depend on the
measure of human observance, all believers know that their
works will be repaid.[50] Either heaven or eternal death will be
the consequence of how they have treated their neighbor.[51] On

---

[50] Mark 9:41; Matt 16:27.
[51] Matt 25:46.

the other hand, those who practice almsgiving, prayer, and fasting to be seen by others "have received their reward."[52] But if you practice these things in secret, "your Father who sees in secret will reward you."[53]

The reward for the good servant is none other than God himself, who transforms those who serve him into his children. In this way one becomes fully oneself.

Synergy

We have been trying to understand how we should respond to the announcement of the good news that "God is coming to save us." We must first welcome the Savior and thereby acknowledge that we are sinners, meaning that we are incapable of saving ourselves. We must then fulfill what Jesus and God require. Now we admit that we are incapable of doing what is demanded of us; this is what St. Paul acknowledges in his letter to the Romans: "sin dwells within me"; "I do not do what I want, but I do the very thing I hate."[54] The Gospel tradition firmly maintains this paradox, which interpreters have struggled to understand.

Saint Bonaventure suggested recognizing two classes of disciples: the "simple," who need to be content to follow the Ten Commandments, and the "perfect," who can strive to live by the "counsels" of poverty, chastity, and obedience. Biblical critics have unanimously rejected this proposal, noting the saying in which Jesus invited every person to "enter by the narrow gate."

According to J. Weiss and A. Schweitzer, however, the words of Jesus must be understood in this way: because it is impossible to live by them in normal times, we must look for a

---

[52] Matt 6:2, 5, 16.
[53] Matt 6:6, 18.
[54] Rom 7:15–23.

practicable kernel. This radical surgery generates a transitional morality (*Interimsethik*) that opens up escape hatches that are justified by a "morality of virtues." It plunks down an idealized portrait of a righteous person and thereby stirs up a sinful conscience, such as the Protestant tradition likes to awaken. The Sermon on the Mount is, in itself, impracticable. As a result, we are invited either to contemplate an illusory ideal or plunge into the depths of guilt. Those who "de-eschatologize" the Sermon on the Mount create a present that is stripped of every connection with the future, so that there are not two kinds of disciples but rather two messages for two different times.

Finally, some recent critics have tried to rehabilitate the category of the future by placing it in the present. According to R. Bultmann, the present must be interpreted in light of "the future in the now." Because the reign of God is breaking in today, we must make up our minds *hic et nunc.* This existential interpretation of the future eliminates any temporal representation of the reign of God. But is it really appropriate to shrink its activity down to the love that God shows us, and to limit the activity of a person to a decision in the present moment? Other critics are correct when they declare that the action of an individual is carried along by the hope of seeing the reign accomplished in the future.

If, therefore, a person acts, it is because he or she has welcomed God and the intention of his reign. The individual "co-acts" with God. Moral conduct does not "deserve" a reward, since there is no connection between cause and effect: a person's action does not produce salvation; the action is rather the fruit of salvation. A person's action strives to express the action of God, from which it flows. If it does not flow from God's action, this is a sign that the reign of God has not been properly welcomed.

A clarification must be offered here, lest we put the two authors of the action on the same level. God's action is of an

entirely different order from a person's action. It does not proceed from human measures; the two do not work together in
that way. They belong to two different worlds, as different as
heaven and earth. This is the paradox of the whole action of
human beings, who must unite in their acting two heteroge-
neous principles.

To appreciate what has just been said, it is necessary to
grasp the rhythmical nature of human existence. I am conditioned by the world outside: the earth depends on the sun; my
life is marked off by day and night, so much so that I am not
the same person when awake as I am when asleep, nor am I the
same in summer and winter. I am dependent on my body, on
my breathing, and on the expansion and contraction that bring
blood to my heart according to the needs of the situation. I am
conditioned by how others see me and how I see myself; I
depend on each person I meet.

Beyond all these things, I am also aware of being in relationship with an *Other,* by whatever name I call him, one who
is beyond me and yet whom I know to be in me more than I am
myself. Such is the presence or absence of this Other, whether
or not I know him as God.

Since this is the way life is, I must take into account and
respect the two facets of my action, not seeking to subordinate
one to the other, which would be the case if I considered welcoming itself as a form of action, for example, by declaring that
my action is in fact a "welcome." I can no more say that my action is a form of sleep than I can say that my charitable activity
is my prayer: this would be to misunderstand the very nature of
divine activity. The Spirit of God cannot be reduced to any
earthly activity.

A person's response is effectively made possible by God,
who acts within history to bring history to its culmination. In
Jesus, God inaugurated this action to a perfect degree, and it
must be realized over the course of time by the activity of

believers. The action of God still needs to be revealed in the
community of the faithful. Jesus is not merely a model; he is the
one *in whom* we can cooperate to establish the reign of God.

Since the salvation offered to us by God-who-reigns is a
free gift to be welcomed, human action is made possible by
God himself. Christian morality does not consist in saying,
"Obey God and you will live!" Rather, it consists in recognizing that "if you live in God, you will act well." The gift of God
precedes and undergirds our action. This action does not derive from an obligation to an exterior law or from the attraction
of a subjective reward. Thus we can dismiss any naive idea of
commerce with God and every illusion of the "merit" of
good actions. All of this assumes that we will not reduce moral
action to our action alone and requires that we respect the action of God. This analysis has acknowledged that our moral
action must be synergy; now it is simply a matter of putting this
into practice.

ACCORDING TO THE GOSPEL OF JOHN

When reaching the Fourth Gospel, the reader enters a
different world. The same question is indeed raised: "One
must respond to God-who-is-coming." But the answer is expressed in a different way.

John disposes of most of the terms used by the Synoptics.
There is no more "conversion" (*metanoia*) to be done, no more
"rich" (*plousios*) to criticize, no more "money" (*argurion*) to
make proper use of, nor "mammon" to condemn. The response is not described with the verb "welcome" (*dechomai*);
there are no more "poor" (*ptōchos*) to describe as blessed, no
more "little children" (*nēpios*) as objects of the divine solicitude,
no mention of "tax collectors" or "prostitutes" inheriting the
reign of God. But all of these terms, of which John seems unaware, are assumed into another perspective: that of people

encountering Jesus, the light who has come into the world. Everything depends on faith, on welcoming Jesus in person.

The Light Invades the Darkness

At the end of his interview with Nicodemus, who does not understand the revelation about the new birth, Jesus confronts the mystery of unbelief. He has just said that "those who do not believe are condemned already, because they have not believed in the name of the only Son of God."[55] Faith in Jesus is the only work that is expected of a person. It has already been said about the Logos that "the world did not know him. . . . [H]is own people did not accept him."[56] Here it is the Logos incarnate who meets the same fate. But why do people reject the light?

> [19]And this is the judgment, that the light has come into the world, and people loved darkness rather than light because their deeds were evil. [20]For all who do evil hate the light and do not come to the light, so that their deeds may not be exposed. [21]But those who do what is true come to the light, so that it may be clearly seen that their deeds have been done in God. (John 3:19–21)

Their first motive sounds like a tautology: they preferred the darkness to the light. But, John says, this was because of their "deeds," which were "evil." There was a worm in the fruit. So, were these evil deeds the cause of their unbelief? To conclude this would be to scorn a constant teaching of Scripture: good conduct is never a prior condition for religious faith. In Judaism, good works are certainly of the highest importance, but properly because they correspond to the law, which

---

[55]John 3:18.
[56]John 1:10–11.

the Jews recognized as the word of God. Righteous acts express the inward religious attitude of the believer.[57]

Our principal difficulty in understanding what John is affirming here comes from the sense in which he uses the term "works." Typically this means good or bad actions, but for John it signifies the fundamental attitude of a person with regard to God who is coming to meet him or her, through the witness of creation and in the person of Jesus of Nazareth, the One whom God has sent. This is specified in the only other passage in John where the question is taken up of how works relate to coming to faith:

> [28]Then they said to him, "What must we do to perform the works of God?" [29]Jesus answered them, "This is the work of God [= this is what pleases God], that you believe in him whom he has sent." (John 6:28–29)

Judaism promoted many works of the law, and Jesus' interlocutors were implicitly asking which ones were most pleasing to God. To all of these works he opposed a single one: faith. The decision of faith is the work par excellence that is expected. Analogously, the rejection of faith can be called a "work," even if the influence of the "father of lies" has intervened. Unbelief is therefore not an inner tendency that separates people into one category or another from birth.

In our consideration of John 3:19 we offered the translation, "their works" were "evil." But it is important not to misunderstand the true sense of the Greek term used to qualify these works. They are described as *ponēra*,[58] "malevolent," a

---

[57]Christians know, thanks to St. Paul, that their works are not righteous unless they express the divine initiative welcomed by faith: Rom 3:27–28; 4:2–5; Gal 2:16; 3:2, 5, 10–12.

[58]Corresponding to the *Poneros*, the "father of lies" (John 8:44).

description whose opposite is not *agatha,* but "done in God" (3:21). These "works" are antecedent to a welcome or refusal of the Son of God. They disclose a religious decision in the form of one's attitude toward the revelation that was made earlier to Israel. Those who are closed to it and to its requirements will not be open to the revelation God is now offering in his Son. Conversely, those who have made this earlier announcement their own will come to the light. They will welcome the eschatological word of the Son of Man.

The word of Jesus concerns not only Israel, but all people, as John's choice of words confirms: "everyone," "the true light" that is present in the world (1:9). To do the truth does not mean to practice a required morality, but to welcome the influence exercised by the word of God that addresses every person through creation or in the history of each nation.

You Must Be Born Again

According to the Synoptics, the poor and little children are at home in the reign of God. We must become like little children again in order to welcome the reign that is coming. The Fourth Gospel transforms the theme of children in its characteristic way. It is no longer a matter of imitating them, of trying to be humble; Jesus imposes a more radical requirement at the very beginning of his dialogue with Nicodemus:

> Very truly, I tell you, no one can see [enter into] the kingdom of God without being begotten from above [of water and of Spirit]. (John 3:3, 5, author's translation)

John uses the term "kingdom of God" to mean "eternal life," that is, the eschatological reign of God. This is the only place in his gospel where John uses this term. In order to become a child of God, one must be reborn, born from above or born again. God must beget one anew. What is needed is not something on one's own part (availability or humility), but rather an action of God himself that imparts life.

The translation proposed here ("to be begotten") emphasizes that what is in view is not just of the result ("being born"), but of God's action.[59] By reversing the role of the individual (who customarily "begets"), John highlights the divine act. Nicodemus reflects on the heavenly revelation of Jesus from an earthly perspective and points out that it is impossible to return to one's mother's womb. This gives Jesus the opportunity to specify that this begetting, like a second birth, is the work of the Spirit.[60]

Jesus adds that "what is born of the flesh is flesh, and what is born of the Spirit is spirit." The believer is thus indwelt by the Spirit and is no longer alone.

This is the new situation: the believer is now filled not just with the life-giving "breath" from the time of creation,[61] but with the Spirit whom Jesus of Nazareth imparts. The light invades the darkness of my being from the moment I believe that Jesus is the One whom the Father has sent. From that moment on, the action of the believer can be the action of God himself. This is what we have been calling "synergy."

The Believer Must Abide in Jesus

Jesus describes the condition of the believer with the verb "abide," particularly at the end of his discourse on the bread of life:

---

[59] Cf. 1:12–13.

[60] It is appropriate to translate "of water and of Spirit" as a hendiadys: "the water that is the Spirit." This allows us to recognize an allusion to Ezekiel: "I will sprinkle clean water upon you. . . . [A] new spirit I will put within you" (Ezek 36:25–27).

[61] Gen 2:7.

> Those who eat my flesh and drink my blood abide in me.
> (John 6:56)

In Wisdom literature, the verb "abide" signifies "adhere closely to."[62] Thus, the one who is nourished by the food of heavenly teaching enters into the divine life. The Word that feeds us is above us; it opens the divine horizon to us and leads us into it. Jesus later adds the image of mutual abiding, of *two* in *one*. This theme has already been treated in chapter 2. The distance that the Synoptic tradition maintains between Jesus and the believer is bridged by this verb "abide." It emphasizes what effort is actually required of the believer: not yet that of acting, but of remaining one with Jesus.

Bearing Fruit

Jesus, however, does not ask the believer to remain immobile; he expects an "action," which he describes with the allegory of the vine.

> [4]Abide in me as I abide in you. Just as the branch cannot bear fruit by itself unless it abides in the vine, neither can you unless you abide in me. [5]I am the vine, you are the branches. Those who abide in me and I in them bear much fruit, because apart from me you can do nothing. [6]Whoever does not abide in me is thrown away like a branch and withers; such branches are gathered, thrown into the fire, and burned. (John 15:4–6)

The allegory of the vine and the branches takes us beyond the discourse on the bread of life. Abiding is not of value simply in itself; it is the means of fruit-bearing. This allegory also allows us to progress from the figure of the Shepherd and his sheep. Both of these highlight the way believers belong to the Son.

---

[62] Prov 9:5.

The sheep know the Shepherd's voice and follow him. He gathers them together and leads them to green pastures.

In this description, the disciple is depicted according to the traditional conception: the disciple follows Jesus and receives from him the joy of eternal salvation. Sheep and Shepherd represent two distinct realities. In the image in John 15, the I of the vine and the You of the branches are still distinct; however, the vine and the branches are not over against one another. The branches are *in* the vine; they exist only by virtue of the vine that bears them. The disciple is transformed from within: the new being is that of the Son. In this way God's intention to create Adam "in his image" is fulfilled.

On the other hand, to ensure that humans and God are never confused with one another, a duality is also expressed. The disciple, who has become, thanks to the Word, a branch of the only true vine, remains a branch only by personal faithfulness, continually renewed. Personal consent is always required.

Thus, while a beneficiary of the action of the Shepherd, the disciple participates in the action of the vine: the disciple who remains grafted onto the vine is the co-author of the fruit that the vine bears. The goal of grafting (15:2) is precisely to maintain a perfect "synergy" between the Son and his disciples.

Answered Prayer

Another result of the disciple's coexistence with the Son is anwered prayer:

> [7]If you abide in me, and my words abide in you, ask for whatever you wish, and it will be done for you. [8]My Father is glorified by this, that you bear much fruit and be my disciples. (John 15:7–8, NRSV, marg.)

Jesus renews the assurance here, which he has already offered in 14:13, that what we desire of God will be granted. In

keeping with the context, we should understand the object of
the request to be the production of fruit, which is intended to
bring glory to the Father.

The Works of a Disciple

Let us return to the problem of the disciple's "action,"
which the allegory of the vine and the branches solved by
showing that the action of the disciple consists in expressing
the action of the Son. Jesus speaks of the same mystery with
the word "works":

> Very truly, I tell you, the one who believes in me will also do
> the works that I do and, in fact, will do greater works than
> these, because I am going to the Father. (John 14:12)

Jesus identifies the action of his disciples with his own action. It is not that he provides a "model" for them to copy slav-
ishly; these words are spoken in a context that clarifies the
character of the imminence of the reign of God. Jesus certainly
calls hisdisciples to an exceptional moral standard, but at the
same time he announces a synergy. The text goes so far as to
declare that the believer will do not just the works that Jesus *has
done,* but those that Jesus is *still doing.* The verb is in the present indicative, meaning that even if Jesus is just about to die, he
will not cease to act for the glory of his Father. We know that he
fulfilled his mission on earth, but he nevertheless continues it
today through his disciples, whose activity expresses his own.

What are these "greater works" spoken of here that the disciples are to perform? The difference does not consist in the
quantity of the works, nor in their nature, but in their degree of accomplishment. The disciples of Jesus are now working together
with him to "gather into one the dispersed children of God."[63]

---

[63] John 11:52.

Conclusion

The two traditions, Synoptic and Johannine, present the same co-action of humans and God, although from different points of view. For the Synoptics, we who know only too well that our actions are "sinful" in themselves need to become like children or like the poor in order to recognize that we can only act as we should through God alone. By welcoming the good news of Jesus, we makes room for God to act. Thus human action becomes synergy with God's action.

The Fourth Gospel upsets this duality between humanity and God in order to highlight the unity of their action: the disciple must "abide" in Jesus in order to bear the fruit that is expected. Jesus' words in the Fourth Gospel might lead some into a type of mystic behavior that no longer respects the duality between the believer and Jesus. But what John does in his gospel is indispensable to keep us from classifying Jesus among the ordinary people of this world.

Both traditions are necessary to describe the appropriate human response to God, who comes in search of us. Human action is to express that of God himself. This might lead us to ask: are humans God? Certainly not, in ourselves. But we are God's image.

Chapter 4

Engaging the Realities of This World

We are not alone. We are in relationship with the universe and with other people.

ACCORDING TO THE SYNOPTIC TRADITION
Being and Having

Confronted with God-who-is-coming, humanity, the "earthlings," the dwellers of the earth, must allow ourselves to be transformed by God in order to act in his image. We remain attached to the earth, from which we derive and through which we can express ourselves. But it is God who has given us our body, that is, the earth. We thus live in a tension between God and the earth, between the being we aspire to become and what we already have as a possession. According to God's plan, the earth was given to us so that we could be nourished by its fruits and so that we could make it bear fruit more abundantly. The earth is good and beautiful, and should be treated with respect, in thanksgiving to its Creator.

The people of Israel experienced in their history a tension between "having" (possessing) and progressing toward "being."

Deuteronomy recalls the condition of the chosen people this
way, as they were marching through the desert toward the promised land, along . . .

> ². . . the long way that the Lord your God has led you these
> forty years in the wilderness, in order to humble you, testing
> you to know what was in your heart. . . . ³He humbled you by
> letting you hunger, then by feeding you with manna, . . . in
> order to make you understand that one does not live by bread
> alone, but by every word that comes from the mouth of the
> Lord. (Deut 8:2–3)

The people of Israel, unfortunately, did not throw themselves
upon the divine mercy that promised them life in abundance.
Instead of trusting in God to take care of them, they gave
themselves over to the concern for obtaining those things they
felt the most immediate need of.

Jesus recapitulated this part of Israel's history when, suffering from hunger in the desert, he resisted the demonic suggestion that he turn stones into bread. Because he thus refused
to subordinate the creation to his own personal needs, Jesus is
presented in this episode as the true Israel.

Echoing this experience, a passage in the Sermon on the
Mount shows that the disciple of Jesus is, for his own part, sus-
ceptible to the tension between being and having:

> ²⁵Therefore I tell you, do not worry about your life, what you
> will eat or what you will drink, or about your body, what you
> will wear. Is not life more than food, and the body more than
> clothing? ²⁶Look at the birds of the air; they neither sow nor
> reap nor gather into barns, and yet your heavenly Father feeds
> them. Are you not of more value than they? ²⁷And can any of
> you by worrying add a single hour to your span of life? ²⁸And
> why do you worry about clothing? Consider the lilies of the
> field, how they grow; they neither toil nor spin, ²⁹yet I tell you,
> even Solomon in all his glory was not clothed like one of these.
> ³⁰But if God so clothes the grass of the field, which is alive

today and tomorrow is thrown into the oven, will he not much more clothe you—you of little faith? [31]Therefore do not worry, saying, "What will we eat?" or "What will we drink?" or "What will we wear?" [32]For it is the Gentiles who strive for all these things; and indeed your heavenly Father knows that you need all these things. [33]But strive first for the kingdom of God and his righteousness, and all these things will be given to you as well. (Matt 6:25–33)

Jesus speaks here to those who are anxious about their duty to provide what is needed for a decent life: food and clothing. The examples he uses are drawn from everyday living, and most of the argument he makes could just as easily have come from a typical Stoic philosopher. The decisive point, however, comes at the end: it is the pagans who are concerned for providing for their own existence; they "strive for these things," while "your heavenly Father knows that you need all these things." He feeds the birds and clothes the grass of the field.

Little by little the opposition that structures this discourse emerges, the opposition between "do not worry" (v. 31), a reprise of the original injunction (v. 25), and "strive" (v. 33), which reprises the striving of v. 32. But the meaning of seeking changes: it is no longer the everyday care for subsistence, but the search for the reign of God.

Jesus does not teach on "do not worry": he does not say that it is not really necessary to be concerned for the necessities of life; he does not tell his disciples to abandon themselves to divine providence, nor to maintain confidence in God by thinking it a duty to lack foresight. He is content to remind them of what faith in God as Creator requires, and by doing just this—which is a lot—he is echoing the Old Testament.

Jesus assumes faith in God as Creator (which is difficult in itself!) and invites his listeners to seek the reign of God. They are to see their desires transformed. They are now to desire more than just becoming fully human: they are to welcome

God, who is pursuing something above creation. That is, they are to welcome God himself working in them. We are always in danger of making the earth, what we "have," our principal concern, while we are called always to desire something more. The earth remains the object of our desire, but heaven calls us to greater things.

The context in Matthew confirms this interpretation. The sayings that precede our passage say this:

> [19]Do not store up for yourselves treasures on earth, where moth and rust consume and where thieves break in and steal; [20]but store up for yourselves treasures in heaven, where neither moth nor rust consumes and where thieves do not break in and steal. [21]For where your treasure is, there your heart will be also. [22]The eye is the lamp of the body. So, if your eye is healthy, your whole body will be full of light; [23]but if your eye is unhealthy, your whole body will be full of darkness. If then the light in you is darkness, how great is the darkness! (Matt 6:19–23)

These collected logia, which were originally independent, interiorize the invitations we have considered above. If they maintain a clear opposition between heaven and earth, this is only to show more clearly that both freedom from worry and an intense pursuit of the reign proceed from a "simplicity" that will accept no mixed motives. They proceed from a loyalty to a single master, that is, from a love that directs one's action.

The Human Person and Money

Jesus' later followers would sometimes think it spiritual to relinquish all of this world's goods. But Jesus showed how well he knew us when he made money a very practical—and very dangerous—means of communication. When money is stored up for its own sake, it tends to become an idol in which we are tempted to trust. And so, on several occasions Jesus warned against the lure of wealth.

An attachment to money can keep us from following Jesus

The love of money can prevent us from committing our lives to Jesus. This is what was taught in the commentary appended to the story of the rich young ruler:

> [21]"If you wish to be perfect, go, sell your possessions, and give the money to the poor, and you will have treasure in heaven; then come, follow me." [22]When the young man heard this word, he went away grieving, for he had many possessions. [23]Then Jesus said to his disciples, "Truly I tell you, it will be hard for a rich person to enter the kingdom of heaven. [24]Again I tell you, it is easier for a camel to go through the eye of a needle than for someone who is rich to enter the kingdom of God." [25]When the disciples heard this, they were greatly astounded and said, "Then who can be saved?" [26]But Jesus looked at them and said, "For mortals it is impossible, but for God all things are possible." (Matt 19:21–26 = Mark 10:21–27 = Luke 18:22–30)

Jesus appears to require everyone who would be "perfect" to renounce all of one's goods and give them to the poor. Origen, Chrysostom, and Basil all went in this direction in their understanding of this saying, although they each softened Jesus' injunction somewhat. Later, under the influence of the desert fathers and Francis of Assisi, the doctrine of the "evangelical counsels" was elaborated. These were poverty, chastity, and obedience. From there, the concept arose that there was a "perfect life," distinct from the ordinary life. The Reformers unanimously opposed this interpretation, but the Catholics maintained it, incorrectly.[1] Fortunately John Paul II himself has rejected the distinction between "commandments" and

---

[1] Cf. *Catéchisme de l'Église catholique* III, no. 2052–2054.

"counsels," stressing that we are all called to the perfection that consists in loving our neighbor.[2]

It is important that we understand several terms in this text correctly. "If you wish to be perfect" does not refer to a possibility, but specifies a condition for obtaining *perfection*. This is not some Hellenistic ideal of knowledge or virtue; it is rather a matter of "keeping the commandments" with the final result of "loving one's neighbor as oneself." Since the young man claims that he has "observed all these things" and adds "What do I still lack?" Jesus invites him to obtain perfection by "selling all that he has and giving it to the poor." To the one who is properly disposed, Jesus proposes the perfect obedience to God that consists in love of neighbor.[3] And he explains, with the help of a proverbial saying,[4] "It is easier for a camel to go through the eye of a needle than for someone who is rich to enter the kingdom of God." Here the camel represents the biggest beast, and the eye of a needle represents the smallest hole possible. The contrast between the two signifies something that is radically impossible, except of course for God.

Jesus does not condemn money as such, but he does warn that we often turn it into "mammon," or unrighteous wealth, when we make it our principal resource. He says this explicitly in the Sermon on the Mount:

> No one can serve two masters; for he will either hate the one and love the other, or be devoted to the one and despise the other. You cannot serve God and Mammon.[5] (Matt 6:24, NRSV, var. = Luke 16:13)

---

[2] John Paul II, *Veritatis Splendor* (Milan: San Paolo, 1994) no. 18.

[3] Following Jerome and St. Thomas (no. 1595); Ceslas Spicq, *Agapè dans le Nouveau Testament* (Paris: Gabalda, 1958), 1:36–37.

[4] Str-B 1:828.

[5] In the *TOB, mammōna* in Matt 6:24 is translated as "money." This is an unfortunate translation, because the term does not simply

The saying is trenchant, coming as it does at the end of a discussion of the treasures that people seek to accumulate.[6] It is clear that earthly riches, unlike heavenly ones, are perishable. The argument is convincing for those whose "eye is healthy" (Matt 6:22), that is, those whose gaze is fixed on God and his law, and who are not morbidly seduced by idols that make them glance in every direction.[7] Such a person will hear a definitive condemnation not of money itself, but of the help that people seek from money that has become unrighteous wealth—mammon.

Those who are rich are in danger of misunderstanding their own condition and of forgetting the poor

The rich young man was invited to strip himself of his riches for two reasons: the riches themselves and their effect on his relationship with others. Two parables in Luke show successively the danger of wealth accumulated for its own sake and of the veil it casts over the world of the poor.

Those who are rich can be so concerned with how well established they are on this earth that they do not realize that they could die any day:

> [16]The land of a rich man produced abundantly. [17]And he thought to himself, "What should I do, for I have no place to store my crops?" [18]Then he said, "I will do this: I will pull down my barns and build larger ones, and there I will store all my grain and my goods. [19]And I will say to my soul, 'Soul, you have ample goods laid up for many years; relax, eat, drink, be

---

designate the base metal, it describes it. According to the experts (except for U. Luz on this text in *Matthew: A Commentary* [trans. J. E. Crouch; ed. H. Koester; Minneapolis, Minn.: Fortress, 2001]), it is related etymologically to the root *'mn,* "that which is certain, that on which one can count, that which lasts."

[6]Matt 6:19–21.

[7]Matt 6:2–3.

merry.'" ²⁰But God said to him, "You fool! This very night your life is being demanded of you. And the things you have prepared, whose will they be?" ²¹So it is with those who store up treasures for themselves but are not rich toward God. (Luke 12:16–21)

This parable criticizes the man who sees nothing beyond the earth, his goods and his own person. He depends on the reserve he has created for himself, not recognizing that he is mortal. He depends on "having," establishing a treasure for himself, when he should be "rich toward God," that is, validate his "being" by listening to the Creator, master of life and death. He has reduced his "soul" to what he has; this means that when he dies, his possessions are not the only thing he will lose.

The other risk inherent in being rich is that of not recognizing the poor.

²⁹There was a rich man who was dressed in purple and fine linen and who feasted sumptuously every day. ²⁰And at his gate lay a poor man named Lazarus, covered with sores, ²¹who longed to satisfy his hunger with what fell from the rich man's table; even the dogs would come and lick his sores. ²²The poor man died and was carried away by the angels to be with Abraham. The rich man also died and was buried. ²³In Hades, where he was being tormented, he looked up and saw Abraham far away with Lazarus by his side. (Luke 16:19–23)

The rich man is not said here to have been bad; nevertheless his wealth prevented him from being aware of his neighbor Lazarus, who was poor. A chasm is thus opened, whose effects will become evident as soon as he dies:

Between you and us a great chasm has been fixed, so that those who might want to pass from here to you cannot do so, and no one can cross from there to us. (Luke 16:26)

As this parable shows us, money stored up for its own sake leads people not to be aware of those who, at the very door of the rich, are dying of hunger.[8]

We should not conclude from this parable, however, that Jesus condemned wealth as such, because it can be put to good use. An anecdote from the life of Jesus shows this clearly.

> [1]He entered Jericho and was passing through it. [2]A man was there named Zacchaeus; he was a chief tax collector and was rich. [3]He was trying to see who Jesus was, but on account of the crowd he could not, because he was short in stature. [4]So he ran ahead and climbed a sycamore tree to see him, because he was going to pass that way. [5]When Jesus came to the place, he looked up and said to him, "Zacchaeus, hurry and come down; for I must stay at your house today." [6]So he hurried down and was happy to welcome him. [7]All who saw it began to grumble and said, "He has gone to be the guest of one who is a sinner." [8]Zacchaeus stood there and said to the Lord, "Look, half of my possessions, Lord, I will give to the poor; and if I have defrauded anyone of anything, I will pay back four times as much." [9]Then Jesus said to him, "Today salvation has come to this house, because he too is a son of Abraham. [10]For the Son of Man came to seek out and to save the lost." (Luke 19:1–10)

This story is recounted in the classic "encounter" pattern. The initiative belongs to Jesus, who states his intention to stay with Zacchaeus. Zacchaeus's response is immediate: he expresses his joyful acceptance through the gift of half his goods. One who was known as a "sinner" thereby shows that he is a genuine son of Abraham by demonstrating that, rich though he is, he does not trust in money, and he remembers the poor.

By condemning mammon, therefore, Jesus does not close the door of the kingdom to the rich, if the rich will be

---

[8]Luke 16:19–31.

concerned for the poor and if they do not depend on "having" to the detriment of that "being" that can only flourish in God.

The Human Person and Sexuality

If there is a universal experience that all people share in addition to death, it is the experience of sexuality. No one is an island. Let us explore the matter further. If my body is in a constitutive relationship with the whole universe, such that I can say without exaggeration that my body extends out to the stars, then I must also recognize that I am in a constitutive relationship with all other people: I am properly a social being.

To Adam, who here represents all of humanity, the Lord God said:

> It is not good that the man should be alone; I will make him a helper as his partner. (Gen 2:18)

Even though Adam gave a name to each of the beasts of the earth that were brought before him, he undoubtedly did not enter into a dialogue with them. Then God "built" a woman from a bit of flesh that he took out of the body of Adam. This time, the man recognized himself in the woman, and the dialogue began:

> This at last is bone of my bones and flesh of my flesh.
> (Gen 2:23)

The editor of the passage draws a consequence from this: the indissoluble character of their union. We recognize here the foundation of social dialogue: by encountering another person—in this case the woman—man becomes an *I*.

While the gospel offers no teaching about the social condition of people, it does present the fundamental principles of life in society. It discusses the relationship that unites man and woman—marriage, which is the basis of society. Jesus was familiar with the biblical heritage. Even if he recognized that the reign of God could call some people to renounce married life,[9] he vigorously defended the permanence of the marital union.[10]

But a breakdown in communication between spouses can lead to a separation; marriage, which is meant to be a union of two beings, often ends up in disunion. Should such a failure be accepted, or must it be rejected? If accepted, what would become of marriage? But if it must be rejected, would this not lead to the oppression of one or both spouses who would find themselves alienated from one another? Jesus took a stance on this, and the tradition has struggled to interpret a saying that we can attribute to the historical Jesus of Nazareth.

Separation and divorce in Judaism

Under the patriarchal system, only the husband had the right to divorce his wife (Flavius Josephus, *Antiquities of the Jews* 15).[11] In order to divorce her, the husband was required to give the wife a certificate authorizing her to remarry. This custom was based on a passage in Deuteronomy:

> [1]Suppose a man enters into marriage with a woman, but she does not please him because he finds something objectionable about her, and so he writes her a certificate of divorce, puts it in her hand, and sends her out of his house; she then leaves his house [2]and goes off to become another man's wife. [3]Then suppose the second man dislikes her, writes her a bill of divorce, puts it in her hand, and sends her out of his house (or the second man who married her dies); [4]her first husband, who sent her away, is not permitted to take her again to be his wife after

---

9 Matt 19:10–12.

10 Matt 19:1–9 and pars.

11 *Encyclopedia Judaica* VI (1972), 123–27; Str-B 1:303–21; Oskar Rühle, ed. *Die Religion in Geschichte und Gegenwart: Handwörterbuch für Theologie und Religionswissenschaft* (3d ed.; Tübingen: Mohr, 1958), 2:316–18.

she has been defiled; for that would be abhorrent to the LORD, and you shall not bring guilt on the land that the LORD your God is giving you as a possession. (Deut 24:1–4)

This complicated formulation is very vague: divorce is authorized when a woman's husband finds "something objectionable about her." These grounds are interpreted many different ways in Jewish tradition, but are typically described as "misconduct." Some examples include going outside without a veil, bathing with men, eating in public, breastfeeding in public, breaking a commandment of the law, making a vow without keeping it, speaking loudly enough for the neighbors to hear, undermining the husband's reputation, not having children, having a hidden bodily defect . . . what has not been thought of to give the husband complete domination of his wife!

New Testament texts on divorce

The New Testament contains multiple interpretations of Jesus' sayings about divorce. Their number testifies to the interest this subject raised. To appreciate the New Testament's perspective we will attempt a close reading of each of the texts, which reflect very different concerns.

To begin with, here is the saying of Jesus himself, transmitted through two different traditions:

Marcan tradition	*Q tradition*
Mark 10:11 = Matt 19:9	**Luke 16:18 = Matt 5:32b**
Whoever divorces his wife	Anyone who divorces his wife
and marries another	and marries another
commits adultery against her.	commits adultery,
	and whoever marries a woman
	divorced from her husband
	commits adultery.

As we are unaware of the context in which these words were originally spoken, it is difficult to specify what meaning

was intended, except that we can recognize Jesus' general opposition to any divorce or second marriage. Let us examine the
contexts in which these words have been placed in the gospel
narratives.

Luke 16:18 places Jesus' saying about divorce right after
his saying that "not one stroke of a letter in the law will be
dropped."[12] It thereby makes marital faithfulness an example
of strict observance of the law. It becomes a moral imperative,
useful as a precaution against pagan excesses. The goal may
also be to situate marriage at the center of Christian ethics, as
the foundation of society.

Mark 10:1–32 inserts this saying in a group of sayings
concerning children and riches, which are transmitted as part
of a catechism for disciples. Jesus' requirements of his followers are extended to the community (which we can tell is Greek-
speaking, from the word-for-word citation of Gen 2:24 from
the Septuagint in Mark 10:8). The teaching of Jesus holds for
the entire community.

Here is a new order, going back to the primitive order of
creation, that is not afraid to sweep aside interpretations that go
in a lax direction. Every divorce contradicts the act of God, who
wants union. Jesus stood up against the current Jewish opinion
that said, "It is permitted for a man to divorce his wife, so long as
he gives her a certificate of divorce." Jesus said instead:

> [6]From the beginning of creation, "God made them male and fe-
> male." [7]"For this reason a man shall leave his father and mother
> and be joined to his wife, [8]and the two shall become one flesh."
> So they are no longer two, but one flesh. [9]Therefore what God
> has joined together, let no one separate. (Mark 10:6–9)

For Jesus, divorce, just like remarriage, was adultery. For
him it violated the rights of the wife, while for the Jews, the

---

[12]Luke 16:17.

husband alone had the right to fidelity. Jesus inverted the prevailing jurisdiction by giving the wife a right over her husband. She who had simply been an "object" of rights now became a "subject" with rights: the woman was to be respected for her own sake. Marriage seals a reciprocal and inalienable bond.

Nevertheless, Jesus was not making a new law here. The formula concerning marriage is no more an imperative than those concerning anger, vows, or adultery in the heart. While the language is certainly legal in form, the idea behind it is to liberate interpersonal relationships from legal strictures such as codified male despotism.

Jesus therefore takes the woman's side—this was his deepest intention. The gospel tradition reflects this tradition: it likes to show Jesus in the company of women.[13] He never shows any suspicion toward them; he recognized clearly the abuses of his time in the treatment of women. If he proposed a new standard for divorce, this was to communicate an authentic understanding of marriage. He gave it its true meaning.

Jesus' saying thus provides a better appreciation of what marriage is, an appreciation that is reflected in the Pauline texts.[14] The patriarchal language (submission of the wife to the husband) is offset by the demand for love and self-giving on the part of the husband, in the image of Christ. The question of divorce becomes a matter of case law.

In *Matt 19:3–9,* the question is asked in a general sense: "Is it lawful for a man to divorce his wife *for any cause?*" This is an allusion to the rabbinic discussion between Shammai and Hillel. In his response, Jesus invokes the Creator, showing immediately that the will of God is beyond any discussion. But in the end a qualification is added to the traditional saying: "except in the case of *porneia,*" "indecency." This last term can be

---

[13] Luke 8:1–3; Mark 14:3–9; 15:40.
[14] Col 3:18–19; Eph 5:21–33.

variously interpreted.[15] The context favors the interpretation of adultery committed by the woman against her husband. Jesus reasserts the function indissolubility of the marital union.

This entire text of *1 Corinthians 7* concerns marriage and divorce. The basic principle is peace. In my opinion, Paul was married, like every rabbi, before his "conversion," but his wife did not want to follow him in the faith and left him. Paul knew what he was talking about: this is where the exception comes from that we call the "Pauline privilege" (1 Cor 7:12–15).

Conclusion

Jesus did not formulate a "law" on the subject of divorce, but he did proclaim the wife's rights, over against the legalized despotism of the husband: the marriage contract involved two parties, not just one. In Mark 10, the Christian community located the foundation of marriage's indissolubility in God's acts as Creator: divorce destroys the original order that existed before Adam's sin.

As the communities multiplied, it became necessary to draw up "rules" for different cases. Concerns for the moral sense[16] or for the legal prescription[17] varyingly predominate.

Jesus' radical intention was softened and took the form of a directive. Paul declared that a marriage could be ended in certain cases for the sake of peace. The qualification Matthew adds shows

---

[15] The meaning of *porneia* is disputed: 1) *Something objectionable,* as in Deut 24:1—divorce would be authorized for a variety of reasons, not specified here. 2) *Adultery,* the unfaithfulness of the wife to her husband. 3) *Unlawful conjugal union,* particularly according to the legislation in Lev 18:6–18, the meaning of which is probably in view in Acts 15:28–29. In this case, Jesus would be forbidding all divorce except in the case of an unlawful union forbidden in Lev 18 (*TOB*).

[16] Luke 16:18; Mark 10:11.

[17] Matt 5:32; 19:9.

that the indissolubility of marriage is a theological axiom that must remain in tension with another postulate, that of the love that people must try to realize concretely, though without always succeeding. This tension is experienced throughout all of life.

Jesus therefore "humanizes" marriage: he makes it the encounter of two people who are able to relate to one another on a basis of equality. He humanizes the institution by situating it in its relation to creation and to love. Jesus does not promulgate a law, and so he leaves each one the task of discerning the appropriate responses to different situations. Marriage is more than an indissoluble union; it makes the couple—which God himself has brought into being—responsible for their own life together before God.

The Human Person and Society

We are not only related to the world, for which we should be concerned, nor only to our spouse, with whom we seek to live in the companionship of love; we are involved in a complex society, in which we are not just a number among many others, but rather an integral part of a whole, with a specific role to play.

The relationships among people

The relationships among people have been well described by the wise, who have compared them to the human body and the relationships of which it is composed:

> For just as the body is one and has many members, and all the members of the body, though many, are one body, so it is with Christ. (1 Cor 12:12)

After developing this comparison at length,[18] Paul immediately adds that there is a better way, that of fraternal love.[19] If people

---

[18] 1 Cor 12:12–26.
[19] 1 Cor 12:31–14:40.

have organized themselves into a society, this has been in order to divide themselves into their respective functions. But the exchange that constitutes society can quickly become domination, in such a way that the fraternal relation is twisted into a "master/slave" relationship. Protected by the aura of authority, it becomes the basis of a social hierarchy. "Power" is exercised imperiously. This exercise of power has as its foundation the inequality of people: there are masters, and there are slaves. The Marxist solution is to dream of a classless society, without a governing structure, with none dominating and none dominated, without violence or alienation—a society of liberty. But we will have to set this paradisiacal dream aside, since it fails to understand that love alone can provide the basis of unity.

The human person in relation to power

Jesus understood the master/slave situation, and he reacted strongly against it by extolling mutual service. We find this in some texts that, while few in number, are fundamental. Following the request of the sons of Zebedee to sit at the right and left hands of Jesus in his glory, Jesus said:

> [42]You know that among the Gentiles those whom they recognize as their rulers lord it over them, and their great ones are tyrants over them. [43]But it is not so among you; but whoever wishes to become great among you must be your servant, [44]and whoever wishes to be first among you must be slave of all. [45]For the Son of Man came not to be served but to serve, and to give his life a ransom for many. (Mark 10:42–45)

> [25]The kings of the Gentiles lord it over them; and those in authority over them are called benefactors. [26]But not so with you; rather the greatest among you must become like the youngest, and the leader like one who serves. [27]For who is greater, the one who is at the table or the one who serves? Is it not the one at the table? But I am among you as one who serves. (Luke 22:25–27)

Two different traditions report Jesus' protest against the disciples' concern to obtain places of honor. According to Mark-Matthew, this came during an episode in Jesus' public ministry, as he was ascending toward Jerusalem. This is historically probable, given the disciples' expectation of an earthly messianic kingdom. According to Luke, the dispute took place at the Last Supper, a context that allowed Jesus to use his own service at the table as an example. In my opinion, Luke 22:27 preserves the original text better than Mark 10:45, which uses the term "ransom."[20]

The same teaching is found during the Galilean period:

[33]Then they came to Capernaum; and when he was in the house he asked them, "What were you arguing about on the way?" [34]But they were silent, for on the way they had argued with one another who was the greatest. [35]He sat down, called the twelve, and said to them, "Whoever wants to be first must be last of all and servant of all." (Mark 9:33–35)

[1]At that time the disciples came to Jesus and asked, "Who is the greatest in the kingdom of heaven?" [2]He called a child, whom he put among them, [3]and said, "Truly I tell you, unless you change and become like children, you will never enter the kingdom of heaven. [4]Whoever becomes humble like this child is the greatest in the kingdom of heaven. [5]Whoever welcomes one such child in my name welcomes me." (Matt 18:1–5)

It is difficult, if not impossible, to discover from these diverse texts, which are drawn from several traditions, what Jesus' original formulation could have been. However, we can be sure of its content from the literary oppositions they all have in common.

---

[20]I have treated this subject in "La mort rédemptrice selon le Nouveau Testament" in *Mort pour nos péchés* (Brussels: Facultés universitaires Saint–Louis, 1976), 11–44.

The "first" (*prōtos*) is the person of high rank; this position is hereditary and hence carries the prestige of antiquity.

The "great" (*megas*) holds power, and to stay in power the person exerts influence and uses violence.

The meaning of the term "servant" (*doulos*) is difficult for us to appreciate; it can range anywhere from slave to trusted servant. The slave is in a state of absolute dependence: an "object" to be used.

The "servant" (*diakonos*) devotes all efforts to the service of another, to whom he or she is subordinate.

The context is that of the kingdom of God, already present in the reign of God, which demands a new way of thinking and living—a veritable revolution. This is what the saying means that we find scattered throughout the gospels:

> All who exalt themselves will be humbled, and those who humble themselves will be exalted. (Luke 14:11; 18:14; Matt 23:12)

This proverb, which we find inserted in different contexts, criticizes the behavior of those who seek the highest position. It is known in the Old Testament tradition[21] and in the Jewish apocrypha.[22] The formula is ancient, but its meaning is modified by the prophets, who envision a universal transformation.

With Jesus, it is not a simple matter of reversal; it expresses as well a solidarity with those who are in a low position, such as commoners and children. It is not a matter of wishing for change, but of changing by putting oneself on the level of the common people, and this not because of the Torah, but because of Jesus, who set us an example by taking on the role of a servant.

---

[21] Prov 18:12; 29:23; Job 22:20; Sir 3:18; 10:20; 11:12–13; Ezek 21:26b; Dan 4:34.

[22] Ahikar 149–50; Basyr 54:10; Hillel, "My abasement is my exaltation, and my exaltation is my abasement."

The structure of the early church

The scriptural data is varied in its interpretation of what Jesus said about church structure. Like every society, the church had to organize itself. We are not directly concerned with the nature of this organization: was it democratic or hierarchical? What does seem certain[23] is that the Christian community did not first have "charismatic" leadership and then "organizational" leadership. We cannot, therefore, appeal to the former as "more original" and thus "truer." Rather, we observe that the church as an institution has always been characterized by the relationship between the "one" and the "many," in one form or another. It is this relationship that is important: not how the church was first organized, or some "ultimate" form it may take, but how the one relates to the many.

The question we must answer is the following: to be faithful to Jesus, how should that "power" be exercised that must necessarily function within the church? In the eyes of Jesus, to have power is to *serve*. But we are always threatened by "perversions" of meaning, such as when the "priesthood" is defined as a "power over the body of Christ." Let us therefore examine some fundamental texts.

Paul. The earliest references to community leadership are expressed by the verb *kopiaō*, "put oneself to a lot of trouble" (work the soil hard).[24] A special role is earned through activities in which all take part. The duty of "being servants of one another" promotes the cohesion of the community. One must be a "slave" like Christ.[25]

---

[23] Cf. Jean Delorme, ed., *Le Ministère et les Ministères selon le Nouveau Testament* (Paris: Seuil, 1974).

[24] 1 Thess 5:12.

[25] Gal 5:13.

Whenever the Christian community is threatened by division,[26] two opposite movements always emerge that "factionalize" the church: psychics and pneumatics, saints and ordinary believers, laity and clergy, clergy and monks, and even today, left and right, progressive and conservative. How can the unity of the community be preserved?

Paul speaks of the *body,* which is *one* but nevertheless has *many* members. Each one of us has our own gift, not for ourselves, but to build up the community. There is not just *one* charism, but *many* charisms that are the common property of *all.*

Paul came to Corinth as a charismatic missionary, with charismatic power. He tells us that parties formed in the name of one gift or another. Thus he affirms that the charisms are many, and that there is solidarity in the mutual recognition of different gifts, and finally that the body of Christ can only be united by the Spirit. He then provides criteria by which the charisms can be evaluated. Their authority is to be measured by how they contribute to the common good.

Matthew organizes the materials in his gospel according to the needs of his church. Chapters 18–20 culminate in the "service" of the Son of Man (20:28), who provides a model for the church. In chapter 23, the authority of the leader loses its ideal character: all are brothers. The concern is not with hierarchical model, but with serving and humbling oneself.

Mark 10:41–44. "It must not be so among you!" Renouncing power is just as important as renouncing one's possessions.

John 13. Footwashing discloses the meaning of the sacrament of the Eucharist.

---

[26] 1 Cor 12.

Conclusions

1. Given the variety of forms the ecclesial community has taken, no one form asserts itself absolutely. A hierarchical structure is among the genuine possibilities; it is not to be preferred above all others, but it is a genuine option.

2. What matters most is that the church be the church of Jesus Christ.

3. Since the reign of God is universal, the church of Jesus Christ is open to all people.

4. Should not the marginal status of the first Christians provide a model for the church as a whole?

5. The ideal of "service" in the renunciation of "power" must shape the church's existence.

ACCORDING TO THE GOSPEL OF JOHN

For John, the "other" is not people in general, but the believing fellow Christian. Jesus was for him not an ordinary person, but the divine Logos expressing itself through Jesus of Nazareth. He came to create a community and to show it how to conduct itself in the midst of a hostile world, and he provided for it a model of loving right to the end, holding nothing back.

It follows that the good news does not include any teaching about one's relationship to possessions, nor about money, nor about how to behave toward one's spouse, nor about life in society. Nevertheless, in writing his gospel John is not unaware of these realities of everyday life. But his purpose is different; it goes to the very root of human action.

The purpose of this gospel is to make the disciple of Jesus an extension of the incarnate Logos:

> This is my commandment, that you love one another as I have loved you. (John 15:12)

This saying repeats the injunction that follows the act of footwashing, by which Jesus showed the symbolic force of his passion:

> For I have set you an example (*hypodeigma*), that you also should do as I have done to you. (John 13:15)

The Greek term *hypodeigma* indicates that Jesus is not simply offering an example to follow in the moral sphere, but teaching that what he has done is a "showing," in a very specific sense: the Father "shows" the Son all that he himself is doing (5:20). This "showing" even has the force of a gift, as the particle *kathōs* indicates: it does not signify simply "as," in the sense of a comparison, but describes a relationship of generation. We might paraphrase Jesus' words this way: "By acting in this way, I enable you to act the same."

Disciples, in other words, should always be functionally and effectively available to serve one another. This availability is just as important as the act of celebrating the Eucharist, because John, who omits the institution of the Lord's Supper, uses its characteristic verb "do" in the command about footwashing. The connection between the two perspectives can be shown by putting the cultural injunction side by side with the covenant injunction:

Do this *in memory of me.*	I have set you an *example,* that you also should do as I have *done* to you.

We can thus recognize the existence of two "memorials" for the Christian.

Each set of instructions is intended to make the Absent One present in the life of the disciple, even though two very different kinds of "doing" are commanded: reproducing what Jesus did when he instituted the Lord's Supper, versus devoting one's life to the service of others. Each action is intended to constitute the disciples of Jesus into a community. If the Eucharist makes the church, the example of footwashing remains the foundational act by which the church is constituted.

John certainly does not replace the Synoptic imperatives, but he reveals the ultimate foundation without which the Christian community would lose its indispensable base: its relationship to Christ.

Chapter 5

At the Heart of Human Action: Love

The moral teaching of Jesus can be summed up succinctly in the precept to love. But it is still necessary to specify in what the act of loving consists. Within human relationships it is not so much a feeling as a welcome of another whose full happiness we desire. Even if it is often marred by a certain egocentrism, this love is disinterested. We know when we are doing something that goes beyond the limits of the kind of instinctual love we feel for members of our family or nation. We are then on the road that can lead us to recognize the work of God himself. In effect, we are being inspired by the God who makes his rain fall on the good and the wicked alike, without worrying about whether the beneficiary deserves it.

Jesus, however, leads beyond the evidence that comes from faith in God as Creator. To those who are certain that God wants us to love one another is granted another certainty:

> Those who say, "I love God," and hate their brothers or sisters, are liars; for those who do not love a brother or sister whom they have seen, cannot love God whom they have not seen. (1 John 4:20)

> Whoever does not love does not know God, for God is love. (1 John 4:8)

Our action toward other people expresses the divine love that is in us. To describe it ideally, it is an attempt to express how we love God.

The preceding chapters have led us to recognize that God takes the initiative in seeking out sinful humanity: what we call forgiveness is the foundation of covenant history. Our experience is that God has approached us unconditionally. We recognize that God has loved us first. Our behavior is therefore determined by that of God himself, who, being love, forgives.

How did Jesus speak of God's forgiveness? This, after all, is the necessary preamble to the announcement that God loves us. In order to love, how must we forgive? This is a prerequisite for expressing love to others. Forgiveness and love for others are thus the two themes we will develop as we explore "love at the heart of human action."

THE GOD OF FORGIVENESS

For an offense to be forgiven, there must be dialogue between the offended and offending parties. But must not a sinful person be "converted" before entering into dialogue with God? We must answer carefully. For the Jews, God would pardon a sinner who repented. With Jesus, something radically new took hold: his teaching recovered the authentic tradition of the Bible, that God chose to grant his forgiveness prior to any initiative on the part of a sinner.

The Jewish Conception of God-Who-Forgives

One of the fundamental teachings of Judaism is the absolute justice of God, but alongside this is a recognition that God is always ready to forgive, as numerous texts affirm unhesitatingly. We may cite first of all Abraham's quaint intercession on behalf of Sodom, by which Lot and his daughters were saved.[1] There is also the example of Moses, whose intercession led God to "change his mind" and not wipe out the Hebrews who, by making a golden calf, had broken the covenant with YHWH.[2] Just before the covenant was renewed, Moses confessed that his people were "stiff-necked," but appealed to the Lord as the one who "forgives iniquity and sin,"[3] since he is, by definition, "the Merciful One."[4] According to Isaiah, he "pardons abundantly" and could not abandon Israel any more than a woman could "forget her nursing child."[5]

If the Israelite could truly trust in God, who was "good and forgiving,"[6] his certainty of forgiveness depended on an as-yet unknown future. It was at the end of time that forgiveness would be complete. As for the present, he needed to strive through faithful works to deserve forgiveness. Pardon and salvation would be granted to the righteous, but also to the sinner who did penance by obeying the Torah.

By proclaiming the good news that God makes the first move, Jesus overturned the convictions of his time. He expressed this primarily through his parables.

---

[1] Gen 18:16–19:29.
[2] Exod 32:11–14.
[3] Exod 34:9.
[4] Exod 34:6.
[5] Isa 49:15; cf. 55:7.
[6] Ps 86:5.

In Search of the Lost Sheep

Two traditions convey the parable of the "recovered sheep" or the "stray sheep."[7] Underlying these two traditions is an original parable whose text is difficult to determine.[8]

> [12]If a shepherd has a hundred sheep, and one of them has gone astray, does he not leave the ninety-nine on the mountains and go in search of the one that went astray? [13]And if he finds it, truly I tell you, he rejoices over it more than over the ninety-nine that never went astray. (Matt 18:12–13)

> [4]Which one of you, having a hundred sheep and losing one of them, does not leave the ninety-nine in the wilderness and go after the one that is lost until he finds it? [5]When he has found it, he lays it on his shoulders and rejoices. [6]And when he comes home, he calls together his friends and neighbors, saying to them, "Rejoice with me, for I have found my sheep that was lost." (Luke 15:4–6)

Luke presents God in search of the lost sinner, while Matthew directs the message to the leaders of the church, for the sake of the "little ones" in their community. A comparative study of the two texts leads to the conclusion that if Luke has better maintained the original intention of the parable, Matthew has nevertheless preserved the text more literally.

But our interest is in the meaning of the parable. Both versions build on the base of a close bond between the shepherd

---

[7] Luke 15:3–7 = Matt 18:10–14.

[8] Here is an attempt at reconstruction by Eta Linnemann, *Gleichnisse Jesu,* 5th ed. (Göttingen: Vandenhoeck & Ruprecht, 1969), which has been adopted by Merklein, 186–92: "If one of you has a hundred sheep, and one of them goes astray, will he not leave the ninety-nine others on the mountain and go look for the one that has gone astray? And when he finds it (truly I say to you) he rejoices more over it than over the ninety-nine others who did not go astray."

and his flock, but diverge from there. Luke underscores the joy of the sheep's welcome home, while Matthew highlights the search for the stray sheep. He even marks off the text with an exhortation to the community:

> So it is not the will of your Father in heaven that one of these little ones should be lost. (Matt 18:14)

This lesson could have been inferred from the text, but it is really only a secondary deduction derived from the parable. Luke's version shows that the real interest is not in the sheep, nor even in the shepherd, but in the joy of the sheep's welcome home:

> [5]He lays it on his shoulders and rejoices. [6]And when he comes home, he calls together his friends and neighbors, saying to them, "Rejoice with me, for I have found my sheep that was lost." (Luke 15:5–6)

Why such joy? The *Gospel of Thomas* finds a reason: this sheep was the most beautiful of the flock. This is not impossible, but nothing of the kind is specified in the text. For his part, Luke concludes, while insisting on conversion:

> Just so, I tell you, there will be more joy in heaven over one sinner who repents than over ninety-nine righteous persons who need no repentance. (Luke 15:7)

Conversion is certainly one meaning of the parable. But is this something that people must do? The shepherd doesn't appeal to anything the sheep has done to justify his celebration.

God rejoices not because the sinner has been converted, but because he has found the sinner. God himself has gone looking for the lost sheep, and it has come home. This is diametrically opposed to Jewish thinking, in which conversion is required for the renewal of the covenant. For Jesus, conversion is actually the result of God's re-establishment of the covenant.

Tax collectors and sinners are not "lost," but "found." The Pharisees ought to have responded to this not with murmurs but with joy, the joy of God himself.

Divine forgiveness precedes conversion: the sinner who welcomes the good news is saved in principle. By visiting and welcoming sinners, Jesus symbolized the behavior of God himself.

The Father of the Prodigal Son

The parable that is often called (incorrectly) the "Prodigal Son" confirms this first truth about God's forgiveness. It consists of two episodes, the story of the prodigal son and the reaction of the older brother.[9] Each one concludes by describing the joy of the father:

> [23]Get the fatted calf and kill it, and let us eat and celebrate; [24]for this son of mine was dead and is alive again; he was lost and is found! (Luke 15:23–24)

> [32]We had to celebrate and rejoice, because this brother of yours was dead and has come to life; he was lost and has been found. (Luke 15:32)

This close parallelism shows that the narrator wanted to construct a single narrative in which the father is the central figure. He rejoices and wants everyone to rejoice over his son who has come home. But what exactly is being celebrated? A careful analysis will allow us to determine this.

Is the prodigal son truly "converted"? Is this what he has in mind when he talks about his need for food and work? Certain preachers speak of his "imperfect contrition," but the narrative seems not to be concerned with this and does not ask the reader to participate in his "conversion." Rather, it emphasizes

[9]Luke 15:12–24 and 15:25–32.

the welcome by which the father expresses his joy at the prodigal's return: "He ran and put his arms around him and kissed him." He listens to his son when he says, "I have sinned against heaven and before you," but when he hears the prodigal declare that he is "no longer worthy to be called your son," he interrupts him and has him clothed with the finest robe, a ring on his finger, and sandals on his feet. He even has the fatted calf brought so they can have a feast.

The reply to the older brother confirms this summons to joy, which is now addressed to all readers, not just to the Pharisees and scribes who had objected to Jesus' behavior: "This fellow welcomes sinners and eats with them" (Luke 15:2). We must rejoice because the hour has come: God is demonstrating his love for sinners unconditionally.

Jesus Welcomes Sinners

Various episodes in the life of Jesus confirm our interpretation of the preceding parables. Jesus wanted to symbolize by his own attitude the disposition of God himself. God does not wait for the conversion of the sinner; he goes looking for the sinner to let him or her know that a new era has begun.

This is what Jesus proclaimed:[10]

1) At the dinner which he attended in the home of Levi the tax collector, in company with other tax collectors and sinners (these being the "little people" with whom Jesus wanted to share table fellowship).

2) The Pharisees were scandalized by what Jesus did.

---

[10] Mark 2:15–17, based on research by R. Pesch, "La parabole du maître qui rentre dans la nuit (Mc 13, 34–36)," in *Mélanges bibliques en hommage au R. P. Béda Rigaux* (ed. Albert-Louis Descamps; Gembloux: Duculot, 1970), 63–87.

3) He responded to his accusers by proclaiming the meaning of his life: I have come to call not the righteous but sinners. (Mark 2:17)

Thus, when he told Zacchaeus he wanted to stay with him, scandalizing the Jews,[11] this "sinner" hastened to re-establish justice by giving half of his goods to the poor. He found himself "submerged in grace,"[12] that is, by God himself, who came to forgive and break bread with tax collectors and sinners. This explains why Jesus was called "the friend of tax collectors and sinners."[13]

Unlimited Forgiveness

Matthew groups together in the second half of his gospel[14] teachings and recommendations intended by Jesus to keep the community of his disciples united. These include in particular the duty of forgiveness between believers.[15] A saying about this in response to a question by Peter has an equivalent in Luke.

> [21]"Lord, if another member of the church sins against me, how often should I forgive? As many as seven times?" [22]Jesus said to him, "Not seven times, but, I tell you, seventy-seven times." (Matt 18:21–22)

> [3]If another disciple sins, you must rebuke the offender, and if there is repentance, you must forgive. [4]And if the same person sins against you seven times a day, and turns back to you seven times and says, "I repent," you must forgive. (Luke 17:3–4)

The number seven already symbolizes completeness, so the number seventy-seven indicates a super-abundance. Jesus' in-

---

[11] Luke 19:1–10.

[12] Joachim Jeremias, *New Testament Theology,* vol. 1: *The Proclamation of Jesus* (English translation, Charles Scribner's Sons, 1971).

[13] Luke 7:33–35 = Matt 11:18–19.

[14] Matt 14–28.

[15] Matt 18–19.

tention is apparently to indicate a number beyond all measure. Taken literally, the injunction seems incapable of realization, but if we assume that the disciple has welcomed the reign of God, it is actually God himself who grants unlimited pardon.

This is what Matthew wanted to show when he adjoined the parable of the Unforgiving Debtor:

> [23]For this reason the kingdom of heaven may be compared to a king who wished to settle accounts with his slaves. [24]When he began the reckoning, one who owed him ten thousand talents was brought to him; [25]and, as he could not pay, his lord ordered him to be sold, together with his wife and children and all his possessions, and payment to be made. [26]So the slave fell on his knees before him, saying, "Have patience with me, and I will pay you everything." [27]And out of pity for him, the lord of that slave released him and forgave him the debt. [28]But that same slave, as he went out, came upon one of his fellow slaves who owed him a hundred denarii; and seizing him by the throat, he said, "Pay what you owe." [29]Then his fellow slave fell down and pleaded with him, "Have patience with me, and I will pay you." [30]But he refused; then he went and threw him into prison until he would pay the debt. [31]When his fellow slaves saw what had happened, they were greatly distressed, and they went and reported to their lord all that had taken place. [32]Then his lord summoned him and said to him, "You wicked slave! I forgave you all that debt because you pleaded with me. [33]Should you not have had mercy on your fellow slave, as I had mercy on you?" [34]And in anger his lord handed him over to be tortured until he would pay his entire debt. (Matt 18:23–34)

The story is built on the contrast between the two scenes: the forgiveness of a large debt and the refusal to forgive a small debt. The disproportion between ten thousand talents[16] and a

---

[16]In today's terms, "ten years' salary for 16,000 workers," *DNT,* 517.

hundred denarii is equivalent to that between an infinite amount and a finite one.

If, as in Jewish parlance, the "lord" represents God, and if, moreover, the expression "I forgave you all that debt" corresponds to the request in the Lord's Prayer, and if, finally, the debt is virtually infinite, then the text clearly wants to evoke God's limitless forgiveness. On the other hand, the small sum that the wicked servant wouldn't forgive his debtor represents the trifling sum that one person can owe another.

This is how things are in the "reign of heaven," as is stated at the beginning of the parable. The king shows the generosity that Jesus has come to proclaim. The reign of God therefore sets the standard for human action, in this case forgiveness, and even more so it is the source of human action, hence the conclusion that Matthew appends:

> So my heavenly Father will also do to every one of you, if you do not forgive your brother or sister from your heart. (Matt 18:35)

One cannot insist on one's rights in any area, no matter how small. Forgiveness is the basis of mutual reconciliation.

The God of Forgiveness

Jesus was an heir of the Jewish belief in a merciful God who would receive repentant sinners. But his experience led him to proclaim that the last days had come and a new era had begun, an era of definitive forgiveness. As a result, it is not the sinner who, by being converted, obtains divine forgiveness; it is God who takes the initiative in offering forgiveness. Also as a result, the sinner's past no longer exists; the covenant is reestablished, opening the way to love.

Henceforth a person can become so profoundly united to God that any action will become that of God himself, or rather, as we will explain, the action of God becomes that of a person, to the extent that one puts no obstacles in the way of divine action.

LOVING

"No one can love who has not been loved."[17] This statement is acceptable when it has God's prior love for us in view,
and in that case it indicates that the true nature of the covenant
has been recognized. God comes to us unconditionally; he
comes to act in us and with us, stirring up our action.

Thus the human action that Jesus requires of his disciples
is possible. We can obey his radical commandments: to love
without holding anything back; to seek the reign of God; to
serve others; to refrain from anger, greed, and lying. In all of
these areas, the law cannot provide the standard for behavior.
Not only is it incapable of saving us, it cannot even describe
what profound things God expects of us. Jesus had to come
and live a human life so that the living God could be rediscov-
ered beneath the letter of the law.

In order to love humanity, God first had to reestablish his
covenant with us, and this meant forgiving. The same thing
holds for human relationships: first we forgive others totally,
then we can love them. In his parables Jesus specified what he
expected of his disciples: to reach out to others, whether this
means the wicked person who oppresses me, or the enemy
whom I must love, or simply the "other," and especially the one
who is suffering, whose neighbor I must be.

With Regard to Those Who Are Wicked

Wickedness has been present since the beginning of the
world, from the time Cain murdered his brother Abel. But
Jesus calls us to a standard of conduct far above that of retribu-
tive justice.

---

[17] "I would not have known how to love the Lord, if he had not
loved me," *"Odes of Solomon 3:3"* in *Écrits apocryphes chrétiens* (ed.
François Bovon and Pierre Geoltrain; Paris: Gallimard, 1997), 682.

³⁸You have heard that it was said, "An eye for an eye and a tooth for a tooth." ³⁹But I say to you, Do not resist an evildoer. But if anyone strikes you on the right cheek, turn the other also; ⁴⁰and if anyone wants to sue you and take your coat, give your cloak as well; ⁴¹and if anyone forces you to go one mile, go also the second mile. ⁴²Give to everyone who begs from you, and do not refuse anyone who wants to borrow from you. (Matt 5:38–42)

²⁹If anyone strikes you on the cheek, offer the other also; and from anyone who takes away your coat do not withhold even your shirt. ³⁰Give to everyone who begs from you; and if anyone takes away your goods, do not ask for them again. (Luke 6:29–30)

When these sayings are isolated, as they appear in Luke's version, they wrench the disciple out of the ordinary way of living. If I am the victim of a wicked person, and I follow these sayings, will I not reinforce an injustice by doubling it? Must I not insist on my rights and thereby triumph over injustice? This is the normal human reaction.

Jesus contradicts this natural instinct and paradoxically invites us to double the injustice. There is no point looking for some hidden agenda, such as that of "heaping burning coals on the head" of the aggressor.[18] Rather than saying that the victim should be motivated by a desire to transform the aggressor into an admirer of his own behavior, is it not more profound to recognize in the other person a desire to satisfy a real need, one that is unfortunately being misdirected? If someone is in need, why not help satisfy this need? The victim then ceases to retain his or her own "point of view," to pursue his or her own interests, to seek justice for himself or herself. The victim rather sees

---

[18] Rom 12:20. The wicked person will be "surprised and troubled to the point of torment by the love that his victim shows him" (*TOB*).

things from the other person's perspective and leaves it up to God to know how to make use of the situation.

The victim's actions in such a case certainly make no sense unless they have their origins in God. Their goal is to bring about an authentic fraternal relationship. Such actions bring us into the universe of love, in which the saints live, whose king is God alone.

Matthew found it appropriate to present these two sayings of Jesus within the "antitheses," which are grouped together near the beginning of the Sermon on the Mount. In this context these sayings become examples of the principle that Jesus opposes to the law of talion:

> But I say to you, Do not resist an evildoer. (Matt 5:39)

The law of talion put a limit on vengeance:

> [23]If any harm follows, then you shall give life for life, [24]eye for eye, tooth for tooth, hand for hand, foot for foot, [25]burn for burn, wound for wound, stripe for stripe. (Exod 21:23–25)

And the law forbade hatred:

> [17]You shall not hate in your heart anyone of your kin; you shall reprove your neighbor, or you will incur guilt yourself. [18]You shall not take vengeance or bear a grudge against any of your people, but you shall love your neighbor as yourself. (Lev 19:17–18)

According to the sage Ben Sira, forgiveness of another person was tied to God's forgiveness:

> Remember the covenant of the Most High, and overlook faults. (Sir 28:7)

Jesus goes well beyond this, declaring that the oppressed person must, in keeping with his own example, recognize his oppressor as a "neighbor." He is not trying to create a body of civil law; that would be the ruin of life in society. That is why, in the examples he gives, he particularizes what he says by using the pronoun "you" rather than "one." We should therefore not take the actions he commends as "models" of behavior.

Even if the saints' lives abound with similar actions, such as those of Francis of Assisi or John of Kenty, for example, it is certain that Jesus was not asking all of his disciples to live heroically. He only required that they not try to resolve human conflicts by insisting on their "rights." That's already quite a lot.

On the other hand, Jesus was not at all interested in formulating a civil code, after the manner of Tolstoy.

With Regard to the Enemy

Luke passes from the wicked to the enemy, or, more properly speaking, he uses the wicked as one particular example of an enemy. Matthew expands the application in the same way: his next antithesis has to do with love for one's enemies.

Matthew 5:44–48	Luke 6:27–28, 36

[44]But I say to you,
Love your enemies and

                   [27]Love your enemies,
                   do good to those who hate you,
                   [28]bless those who curse you,

pray for those who persecute you, pray for those who abuse you.
[45]so that you may be children
of your Father in heaven;
for he makes his sun rise
on the evil and on the good,
and sends rain on the righteous and
on the unrighteous.
[46]For if you love those who love
you, what reward do you have?
Do not even the tax collectors do
the same? [47]And if you greet only
your brothers and sisters, what
more are you doing than others? Do
not even the Gentiles do the same?

[48]Be perfect, therefore, as your heavenly Father is perfect.	[36]Be merciful, just as your Father is merciful.

The commandment to love your enemies, is clearly anticipated in the First Testament:

> [4]When you come upon your enemy's ox or donkey going astray, you shall bring it back. [5]When you see the donkey of one who hates you lying under its burden and you would hold back from setting it free, you must help to set it free. (Exod 23:4–5)

This being the case, how could Jesus have added, "You have heard that it was said, 'You shall love your neighbor *and hate your enemy*" (Matt 5:43)? Has Matthew generalized in order to create a more radical contrast? The phrase is not, in fact, found in the Torah, but the oral tradition could certainly have sent people's thinking in this direction. At Qumran, there was supposed to be "collective opposition" to all those who did not keep the law.

It would be naive to think that this commandment of Jesus is practicable. We should remember that it contradicts human nature. Even though it is stated as an imperative, we should nevertheless observe that Jesus does not ask us to make the enemy our friend. Rather, he requires his disciple to take on the attitude of God himself, who does not reserve his goodness for the righteous alone, but extends it to all people without distinction, forgiving prior to every conversion. In the same way, disciples of Jesus must express our true nature as "children of the heavenly Father" and let God's love show itself in us toward those whom we consider our enemies.[19]

---

[19]The only other possible conclusion is to make appeal to the following observation: the verb used here, *agapaō,* indicates not natural love (*phileō*), but the love that God stirs up in people. This comment is based on the Gospel of John. Cf. *Lecture de l'evangile selon Jean,* 4:289–90.

In Luke the commandment is detailed: "those who hate you, curse you, abuse you." These details are not exhaustive and leave plenty of room for the general notion of "enemies." In the Bible a person is always confronted by an enemy,[20] a mysterious presence associated with sin and with Satan, the enemy par excellence who was defeated by Christ and who will be defeated by the disciples' love, which expresses the love of God himself. Leaving the "enemy" indeterminate prevents all casuistry, in the same way that the identity of one's "neighbor" is not specified any more precisely. By loving in a divine way those who oppose me, I reach into their inner being and perhaps provoke them to question themselves, through my profound solidarity with them.

Thus the commandment makes sense: "*Be merciful* as your Father is merciful." This is Luke's wording, which legitimately expands Jesus' call to love one's enemies. Matthew expresses the same thought by means of the term "perfect" (*teleioi*), which specifies that the essence of godliness is to exceed the limits we impose on love. The disciple will thus go to the ends of love. This is the same thing that John wanted to express when he said that Jesus, in going to his passion, "loved his disciples to the end."[21]

These considerations should encourage the disciple to "do the extraordinary," beyond the behavior of the heathen, who, for their part, "love those who love them." The disciple of Jesus is not to remain on the level of commercial justice, of equivalent exchange. He listens to God, whose nature is radical kindness, without limit.

Is the commandment to love one's enemies practicable? The answer is yes, if God is already reigning in an individual, stirring up that *agape,* which can alone surpass human limits and which is confident in God, who will one day be victorious

---

[20] Cf. for example P. Beauchamp in *VTB,* 356–59.
[21] *eis telos* (John 13:1).

over hatred. Faith in the Lord Jesus anticipates this day: did he not announce that God reigns even now?

With Regard to Others

Even as I acknowledge that I am surrounded by people who wish me harm, or who want to exploit me by taking advantage of my weakness or naivete, I must also recognize that there are people who are, for me, simply "others." What should be, in general, my behavior toward those who are "other" than I? Can I be indifferent toward them? Do I not have a certain responsibility for them, even if I cannot be concerned about every person in the world? Am I not responsible to some extent for my brothers and sisters, no matter who they might be, and no matter what their situation in life? Do I really have to feel concerned for every potential "brother" or "sister" who is out there?

This question did not escape Jesus of Nazareth. It is raised in the Inaugural Discourse, in a saying that Matthew presents individually and Luke places in the context of loving one's enemies.

Matt 7:12	Luke 6:31
In everything do to others	Do to others
as you would have them do to you;	as you would have them do to you.
for this is the law and the prophets.	

Such a maxim[22] is known from earliest antiquity, in the Greco-Roman world and in Hellenism as well as in Jewish circles.[23] There is nothing specifically Christian about it. Why

---

[22] Some critics (such as Merklein, 243) have attempted to reconstruct the original words of Jesus: "As you wish men to act towards you, act towards them yourselves."

[23] Tob 4:15; *Letter of Aristeus* 207; *Testament of Naphthali* 1:6 (cf. Str-B 1:460); in Philo, and even in negative form in some readings of Acts 15:20, 29.

then, and in what sense, did Jesus retain it? This is what we must seek to determine.

The statement would appear at first to mean, "I should do for the other what I would like him to do for me." But should this "me" really be the criterion by which we determine what good to do for the other? Is such egocentrism really a suitable measure of what there is to be done? Yes, in one sense: I must do good to another according to the good that I wish for myself. I seek the good of another to the extent of my understanding of what is good for me. Another person's good is thereby identical to the good I wish for myself.

This creates an acute sense of the communion of beings. Certainly the other is not me, but he or she is "another me." To the extent that I understand myself, I will accordingly seek for the other the same good as for myself. By adding "this is the law and the prophets," Matthew comments, "this is the law Jesus understood."

Having had the experience of God who reigns and saves now, who is perfectly oriented toward people, Jesus declares that the "me" should be oriented toward the other.

And Who Is My Neighbor?

Jesus invites his disciple to regard the other as oneself, but did he really give an answer to the scribe's question, "And who is my neighbor?" A careful reading of the parable known as the "Good Samaritan" will allow us to determine this.

To whom is the reader's attention drawn: is it to the wounded man rather than to the priest or the Levite? One traditional interpretation of this parable identifies the Christian with the wounded man who is waiting for help, counting on some assistance being brought to him, who finds himself disappointed until, contrary to all expectations, he is helped not by one of the religious leaders among his fellow Jews, but by a layperson who is a foreigner. Understood in this sense, the parable seeks to enlarge the Christian's horizon, beyond religious boundaries.

Another reading invites me to draw near to the wounded man myself. But in what way does this go beyond the behavior that we have a right to expect from anyone faced with a wounded person? Does this not simply bring us back to the universal law that renders anyone culpable who does not help a person who is in danger?

Finally, let us specify what the text says in its entirety: Jesus does not show the scribe who his neighbor is; rather, he puts a different question to him:

> Which of these three, do you think, was a neighbor to the man who fell into the hands of the robbers? (Luke 10:36)

In other words, Jesus turns the question back to the scribe. The "other" cannot be designated; *you* are the one in view. It is *you* who must draw near to the wounded man *yourself.* You must make *yourself* the neighbor. You cannot determine who this "other" is, who is always at hand, but you can become a neighbor when the occasion presents. Jesus gives us some more information about what this "occasion" is in the parable of the Last Judgment.

Your Neighbor Is the "Least of These" in Difficulty (Matt 25:31–46)

> [34]Then the king will say to those at his right hand, "Come, you that are blessed by my Father, inherit the kingdom prepared for you from the foundation of the world; [35]for I was hungry and you gave me food, I was thirsty and you gave me something to drink, I was a stranger and you welcomed me, [36]I was naked and you gave me clothing, I was sick and you took care of me, I was in prison and you visited me." [37]Then the righteous will answer him, "Lord, when was it that we saw you

hungry and gave you food, or thirsty and gave you something to drink? [38]And when was it that we saw you a stranger and welcomed you, or naked and gave you clothing? [39]And when was it that we saw you sick or in prison and visited you?" [40]And the king will answer them, "Truly I tell you, just as you did it to one of the least of these who are members of my family, you did it to me." (Matt 25:34–40)

In this text, which is describing the Last Judgment, it is remarkable that the sole criterion of judgment is a person's conduct toward others, rather than any religious decision he or she has made.

The "righteous" draw near to help the "least of these" (who, according to the most widely accepted interpretation, are people in general, and not just disciples of Jesus[24]) because they perceive that any person in difficulty is a "neighbor" and that this neighbor is Jesus in person. To love other people is to love Jesus the Lord.

CONCLUSION

This last chapter has been intended to draw together the elements scattered throughout the preceding studies. The conclusion is that we always find ourselves in the presence of the "other." The Christian discovers that this other, whom I wish to engage, is Jesus himself, even though I do not recognize him immediately. Unfortunately, I am too concerned with my own being to make the other the center of my vision of the world. I have to forget myself—in that way I will discover in the end what I sensed in advance, that my action in reality is not mine, but the action of God himself.

---

[24]Certain interpreters hold that the "least of these" are oppressed disciples of Jesus, whom pagans have helped.

Epilogue

Let us . see if we can gather up the fruits of our inquiry. Have I identified the principle of our moral action?

1. God has burst into human moral action. Having recognized that nothing but evil can spring from the sinful human person in itself, apart from God, I acknowledge that the good that is in me and the good that comes from me actually comes from an Other than myself—from God himself. It is time to take seriously the mystery of the covenant, which was restored definitively by the One who inaugurated it and who today is bringing it to its proper culmination. When Jesus announced that the "reign of God is here," he was declaring his experience of the presence of God, Israel's Savior. He expressed this experience not by repairing an edifice that sin would have destroyed, but by going back to the beginnings of the plan of God, who wanted to make people his own children. This is the meaning of the name *Abba,* by which all people are invited to address God:

the forgiveness of God, prior to all human action, re-establishes the covenant.

Can this experience of Jesus become my own? The Synoptic tradition presents Jesus as a question and shows that Jesus, by saying, "Follow me," wanted to communicate his own life and his own example to his disciples. The Fourth Gospel shows me that the disciple must "abide in him." We must do more than follow and imitate Jesus; we are called to express the love that Jesus himself manifested, the love of God the Father. Like a prophet, therefore, I have the honor and the responsibility of expressing God himself.

2. It would be naive to say that the reference to the "reign of God" dispenses with the law. Saint Paul, who insisted so much on the "end of the law," did not hesitate to speak of the "law of Christ," as if the Torah had come back to life in the law of Christ. The disciple of Jesus does not become a libertine; the criterion of one's action is henceforth the word of Jesus in his gospel. Following this word is only possible through the Holy Spirit, who is spoken of in the Fourth Gospel, the culmination of the gospel tradition. The Paraclete is the presence of the risen Christ himself. Thus, by listening to the Spirit, the disciple lives by the gospel not as a dead letter but as the living Word.

The other criterion of my action is the "other," the one whom I meet on the way. I am called to "draw near" to the "other," who thus ceases to be a being who is "other" and becomes, in a sense, another me.

3. If this is the case, then human moral action is a divine action, what we might call the synergy of human and God. Thus anthropology is transformed: humans are already beings dependent on God for every breath. This

must be universally recognized, to the extent that one recognizes that humanity has moved beyond being just human and has taken on the imprint of Another. But now, with the coming of Christ, the breath of God continually animates the believer.

I thus recognize that my being has a double dimension. There is a rhythm to my existence, and it is not just the rhythm of day and night, work and rest, waking and sleeping. Action presumes a welcome, and it is the two of these together that constitute my being. I cannot reduce the welcome to an action; the welcome is not simply a way of getting into action; I validate the welcome when I am able to see the action in its symbolic dimension.

4. I will conclude my inquiry into acting according to the gospel by citing St. Augustine, who has given me a key to unlock the mystery of the relationship between divine grace and my own free will. God and humanity are not two co-participants in spiritual activity, but they each have their role. There can be conflict between them, but not sharing. In religious behavior, and even in general, humanity does not "let God do his part." We confess that God accomplishes everything, but we also know that we play an inexpressible role: we welcome the gift of God.

Augustine, the man who emphasized that it is God alone who acts, nevertheless warned the monks of Hadrumetum, who derived from his statements an invitation to be completely passive without acting, on the pretext that the Holy Spirit was acting in them. In the following quotation, it is important to note how often the verb "to act" is repeated:

Let them rather understand that, if they are the children of God, they are acted upon by the Spirit of God, so that they act

what they should act, and when they have acted, let them give
thanks (*gratias agant*) to the one through whom they act. They
are acted upon in order to act, not in order not to act.

Act . . . act . . . prayer must help them in their conduct of Christian warfare:

> When they are not acting, let them pray to receive what they
> do not yet have. What shall they have that they shall not have
> received? Indeed, what do they have that they have not re-
> ceived?

But it would be no less grave a mistake to use these texts
to establish a human activism. It is indeed we who possess our
souls by our patience. But if this patience is ours, it is because
God has given it to us: "That is ours which comes from us; that
is ours also which is given to us (*illo dante fit nostrum*)."

Everything is a gift of God, but everything is human action: *da quod jubes et jube quod vis!* May our activity thus be animated by prayer: always act, but in praying. Augustine in no
way misunderstood the necessity of action, but he was jealous
for the glory of God and thus attacked the arrogant character of
action that thought itself independent.

Could anyone better express the mystery of human action?

Subject Index